MONSON
Free Library and Reading Room
ASSOCIATION

NO.   51213

RULES AND REGULATIONS

Assessed fines shall be paid by every person keeping Library materials beyond the specified time.

Every person who borrows Library materials shall be responsible for all loss or damage to same while they are out in his name.

All library materials shall be returned to the Library on the call of the Librarian or Directors.

General Laws of Mass., Chap. 266, Sec. 99

Whoever willfully and maliciously or wantonly and without cause writes upon, injures, defaces, tears or destroys a book, plate, picture, engraving or statute belonging to a law, town, city or other public library shall be punished by a fine of not less than five nor more than fifty dollars, or by imprisonment in the jail not exceeding six months.

A New Library of
the Supernatural

Monsters and Mythic Beasts

Monsters and Mythic Beasts

by Angus Hall

Doubleday and Company, Inc.
Garden City, New York, 1976

Series Coordinator: John Mason
Design Director: Günter Radtke
Picture Editor: Peter Cook
Editor: Sally Burningham
Copy Editor: Mitzi Bales
Research: Marian Pullen
General Consultant: Beppie Harrison

Library of Congress Cataloging in Publication Data
Hall, Angus
Monsters and Mythic Beasts
(A New Library of the Supernatural; v. 6)
1. Monsters   2. Animals, Mythical   I. Title
II. Series
QL89 H35   001.9'44   75-26141
ISBN 0-385-11312-9

Doubleday and Company
ISBN: 0-385-11312-9

Library of Congress Catalog
Card No. 75-26141

A New Library of the Supernatural
ISBN: 11327-7

© 1975 Aldus Books Limited, London

Printed and bound in Italy by
Amilcare Pizzi S.p.A.
Cinisello Balsamo (Milano)

**Frontispiece: mermaids and mermen at play in the sea.
Above: the Greek hero Jason encounters a sea monster.**

EDITORIAL CONSULTANTS:

COLIN WILSON
DR. CHRISTOPHER EVANS

When we are children the world seems infinitely wide and filled with endless wonders. As we grow older we like to believe that science has taken command of our environment, that the living creatures are classified and the trackless wastes mapped. However, there is much of our earth that is barely known, and from such mysterious places come persistent stories of fantastic beasts—some of which have been told since man was man. A few, like the dragon, the mermaid and the unicorn, seem clearly fictional. But what about huge sea serpents, giant Bigfeet or Yeti, monsters of the lakes? Have a few prehistoric creatures survived in unexplored pockets of inaccessible places to this very day? The evidence is both abundant and curiously mixed. Will we ever have all the answers? Do we want to?

1

Dragons in Myth and Mind

The dragon is probably the most widely known of all monsters and mythic beasts. For centuries, all over the world, it has played a role in art, in myth, and in religion. St. George and the dragon is only one of many legends about this symbolic creature. One version of the St. George myth has it that the people of the North African city of Silene, in what is now Libya, had lived for a long time in fear of an evil dragon outside their gates. At first they had placated it each day with several sheep, but soon it was demanding both a man and a sheep. Then, not content with this, it wanted more delectable flesh and insisted on the sacrifice of young

The dragon is a fine and fabulous beast, flicking his reptilian tail far and wide across the world, at home on the banners of a medieval army riding gallantly into battle or in the splendors of the sumptuous Chinese courts. Above: a fake dragon probably dating from the 16th century when such fakes often appeared in Europe. This one more than likely started life as a harmless little tree lizard found in Java and known as a "flying dragon." Being only about four inches long, it was said to be a "dragon baby." The wings would be parts of bats' wings cunningly sewn into place. Right: the romantic view of St. George rescuing the beautiful princess from the dragon was a popular subject of paintings in the Middle Ages. This one was by a 15th-century Flemish artist.

"Universal symbolic significance"

Below: a chapel altar painting by Albrecht Dürer in 1505 shows St. George with the dragon he slew. In this legend, St. George's killing of the dragon is symbolic of Christianity's superiority to Paganism and victory over evil.

virgins. The king decided that the young girls of the city should draw lots each day to determine who would be the next victim. One day to his horror the lot fell to his daughter, the beautiful Princess Sabra. In vain the king pleaded with his subjects for her life. They were adamant. He must abide by the rule that he himself had made.

Sick at heart, the king saw his beloved daughter led off to the spot where the dragon was eagerly waiting. But at that moment a strange knight appeared on horseback. It was George of Lydda, on his way to see the Roman Emperor Diocletian and plead for the lives of Christian slaves. Making the sign of the cross with his sword, he spurred his horse against the dragon. They fought until the beast fell wounded to the ground. George told the princess to fasten her belt around the dragon's neck and lead it into Silene. The people honored George as a hero, and when he told them he had been made powerful by the Christian God, they accepted Christianity. George then took his sword and cut off the dragon's head. By an odd coincidence the town of Silene is near the place that Perseus, a hero of Greek mythology, is said to have rescued the beautiful Andromeda from a terrifying sea dragon.

The fight between St. George and the dragon is usually interpreted as an allegory showing the triumph of Christianity over the powers of darkness. But legends and traditions found in many different places show that this struggle had an earlier and more universal symbolic significance. In countries as far apart as

China and England we find that the dragon, from early times, represented the principle of fertility. He was born each spring from an egg underneath the water and, like Nature at that season, he grew and flourished. Each year as Nature waned the old dragon had to be killed to make way for the new dragon that would be born the following spring. When in the Western Christian tradition the dragon became synonymous with evil, the killing came to symbolize not merely the end of the year, but also the victory of God over the Devil. The slaying of the dragon for this reason has been associated with many Christian saints besides St. George, and with secular figures as well.

Modern psychology takes still another view of the dragon myth. The struggle with the dragon has been interpreted as symbolizing our own internal struggle between deep-seated lusts and unconscious drives on the one hand, and the demands of conscience on the other. The fertility legend is likewise given a new slant. The dragon is seen as the old man or father whose sexual potency has diminished, and who must be killed by the vigorous young sons so that they can take over the sexual role and enable life to continue. Another psychological interpretation springs from the role the dragon has in many legends as guardian of treasure. In this case the treasure is seen either as the son's sexual drives, to be guarded or restrained by the mother in the role of dragon, or as the daughter's virginity, to be preserved by her father in the dragon role.

Below: an Italian artist's version of the St. George legend in about 1502. The earliest stories about St. George made him a Christian martyr of the 4th century in North Africa. During the first crusades the nature of his character changed, and he became a warrior-saint in knight's armor. The first trace of his legendary battle with the dragon to save the life of the princess appeared early in the 13th century. In these accounts he was offered the princess and the kingdom as a reward, but nobly refused and rode off to do more good deeds. Some later accounts, however, have him marrying the princess Sabra and going to live happily in England.

In contrast to the West, the dragon in China is the embodiment of gentleness and goodwill. The Chinese dragon legends and interpretations therefore differ greatly. But whatever the symbolism, why should these strange hybrid creatures exert such power and fascination over our minds? There are land dragons, water dragons, flying dragons, fierce and timid dragons. There are dragons of many shapes in nearly every part of the world. Where do they spring from? Were they created to fulfill some deep need in humans, to personify the otherwise inexplicable forces of Nature, to provide some explanation for arbitrary fate? It seems that this might have been so. But while the West took the dragon to symbolize the evil, ungovernable, and destructive side of Nature, the East used it to portray the life-giving, benevolent, and restorative side. Both aspects were equally incomprehensible and mysterious, and lent themselves to interpretation by symbols

Left: *Perseus and Andromeda* by Italian Renaissance artist Piero di Cosimo. In the Greek myth on which this is based, Andromeda is left fastened to the rocks as a sacrifice to a sea dragon which has been ravaging her homeland of Ethiopia. Perseus rescues her with his magic weapons, and takes her as his wife. With this story the Greeks added a new element to the dragon legend: that the beast could be appeased by the sacrifice of a virgin, most often a royal princess. It was probably this story that later was shaped in Christian terms to become the legend of brave St. George and the dragon. Below: this is how one medieval miniature painter envisioned the rescue of Andromeda by Perseus.

that made them easier to understand for ordinary people.

Just as our early ancestors endowed many of the gods with a mixture of human and animal attributes to make them more powerful than either humans or animals, so they may have conceived of dragons as a mixture of different creatures in order to suggest their supernatural power. It seems that, just as different peoples interpreted the character of dragons to fulfill their own needs, so they concocted the appearance of the dragon from the beasts they found most significant. Thus in India we find an elephant dragon, in China a stag dragon, and in Western Europe —where the dragon myths stem from those of the serpent—we find a reptilian dragon. The Western dragon is so reminiscent of prehistoric reptiles that one is led to wonder whether the conception stems from folk memories of giant dinosaur fossils, or even a late freak survival of a prehistoric monster.

Since the serpent was in many civilizations the ancestor of the dragon, we find that in many myths the identity of the two creatures overlaps. The serpent sometimes becomes a dragon in later phases of the same legend. One of the first dragons to appear in myth is thought to be Zu. He arises in the legends of the Sumerians who settled in Mesopotamia possibly as early as 5000 B.C. The dragon Zu was said to have stolen tablets setting out the laws of the universe from the chief god of the Sumerians, Enlil. As a punishment Enlil ordered the sun god, Ninurta, to kill the dragon. This battle between the dragon and the sun god is repeated in the myths of many later civilizations, and seems to symbolize the struggle between light and darkness, between good and evil.

When in about 1800 B.C. the Babylonians gradually replaced the Sumerians as a leading power, they took over many of the Sumerian myths. Their story of creation is the story of the struggle between order and chaos, good and evil. The forces of chaos are personified by the sea goddess Tiamat, who adopted a dragon for her symbol. She led a fierce army that included serpents and dragons with crowns of flame, and attacked the gods, who stood for order. The dragon, representing Tiamat, was therefore associated with forces of destruction. Marduk, the

Below: a depiction of the battle in heaven between Archangel Michael and a dragon, described in the New Testament book of Revelation. The dragon, which was the Devil in this case, was overcome by the forces of good.

chief god of the Babylonians and god of the sun, was determined to fight Tiamat in single combat. He used the winds as his main weapon. When Tiamat opened her mouth to consume him, he drove the winds into her mouth and body. Her body became distended and she was unable to close her mouth. Marduk then shot an arrow down her throat, killed her, and severed her body in half. One half became the earth and the other the heavens. Thus the dragon is involved in the myth of creation.

Babylonian and Sumerian ideas spread to Egypt, and probably inspired the legend of the enormous serpent Apophis, the enemy of the Egyptian sun god. Later this serpent became identified with the ocean, which in Egyptian myth held the world together but constantly threatened to destroy it. Then the myth developed into the struggle between night and day, light and darkness. In some versions the serpent or dragon, representing night, swallowed the sun at sunset and disgorged it the next morning. In others the sun went down to the underworld each night to fight the dragon and, having each time succeeded in hacking him to pieces, came up to earth again in the morning. Throughout the West and Middle East dragons were generally regarded as carriers of evil and bad luck. They might vary greatly in appearance—some resembling serpents, others being formed from such

Below: this medieval tapestry shows the seven-headed dragon that, according to St. John's book of Revelation, menaced the earth after being cast out of heaven. It is sometimes called the Great Beast of the Apocalypse.

In the Far East the dragon is a benevolent creature associated with prosperity and good luck.

Right: this rich silk robe with an embroidered dragon was made for an 18th-century Chinese ruler. The dragon motif was a favorite one among the Chinese emperors.

Left: illuminated to glow across the water, this giant sea dragon was part of the festivities held in Singapore to mark the 1953 coronation of Queen Elizabeth II.

Below: the coronation dragon's head in close up shows its huge size and intricate construction.

unlikely combinations as a lion, a crocodile, and a hippopotamus —but they nearly all have a common characteristic: an endless hostility against human beings.

Some Western medieval scholars believed that the majority of dragons lived beneath the earth in an area honeycombed with caves. Dragons preferred to be underground, and the only ones seen above ground were those that had somehow gotten lost and strayed into the world of sky and sunshine. Unable to find their way back, they vented their frustration on any person nearby. In psychological terms, the dragons from the dark depths become the evil thoughts dwelling in all of us which, once they are allowed out into the open, bring trouble, pain, and sometimes death to our fellow beings.

It was an early dream expert, the 2nd-century Greek Artemidorus, who first mentioned dragons in connection with guarding treasure. He believed that dragons were to be found where treasure was hidden, and that therefore dreams about dragons signified riches and wealth. The link between dragons and treasure, and the caves where treasure was usually hidden, is found in many legends in different countries. It became a popular theme in the early Christian and the medieval periods, probably because it lent itself to many symbolic interpretations. In the Teutonic legend of Siegfried, for example, the dragon watches over a hoard of treasure that is the source of life. Siegfried acquires invulnerability by bathing in the dragon's blood after he has killed it. Also by drinking the dragon's blood he learns the language of the birds. In other words, he gains a new understanding of Nature. In many other legends the heroes gain new kinds of power from killing and eating parts of the dragon.

The English writer J. R. R. Tolkien gives a vivid picture of a dragon as treasure keeper in his modern fable of the struggle between good and evil, *The Hobbit*. He calls the beast Smaug and describes him this way: "There he lay, a vast red-golden dragon, fast asleep; a thrumming came from his jaws and nostrils, and wisps of smoke . . . Beneath him, under all his limbs and his huge coiled tail . . . lay countless piles of precious things . . ."

Britain has many dragon legends. One they owe to the Danish invaders of the mid-6th century, who brought with them their epic of King Beowulf. Although he beheads the murderous monster Grendel, Beowulf is killed by a dragon whose treasure has been stolen. An even earlier folk story concerns the legendary British monarch King Lludd, who lived happily in the city he had built in the southeast of the island—a city later called Londinium by the Romans and London by the Saxons. Suddenly peace was destroyed by an evil that "went through people's hearts, and so scared them, that the men lost their hue and strength, and the women their children, and the young men and the maidens lost their senses, and all the animals and trees and earth were left barren."

King Lludd sought the advice of his older brother, King Llevelys of France. "The plague in your kingdom is caused by a red dragon," King Llevelys said. "Another dragon of a foreign race is fighting with it, and striving to overcome it. And therefore does your dragon make a fearful outcry." King Llevelys gave King Lludd careful instructions about how to rid his land of the

Opposite: according to English legend, the Yorkshire knight Moore of Warncliffe killed the dreaded Dragon of Wantley. Then, in keeping with the romantic ideas of the age of chivalry, he demanded a fair young maiden as reward.

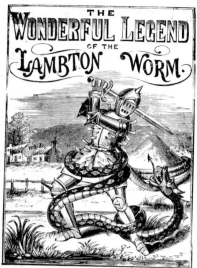

Above: the title page of an 1875 book on the Lambton Worm, one of the most popular and persistent English dragon stories. There is no beautiful damsel involved in this legend of a young lord who overcame the huge worm by following a witch's advice and wearing armor studded with blades to cut up the monster. This old tale also has the twist of a family curse brought about because the knight unwittingly breaks a vow.

Below: the red dragon of the Welsh flag. It is thought that dragons may have once been used on flags carried in battle as a kind of psychological warfare to give the enemy an added fright.

monsters. King Lludd returned home and, following his brother's directions, had a pit dug in the exact center of his domain. As Llevelys had predicted, the dragons grew tired of battling one night, and fell exhausted into the pit. They drank the mead that had been poured in and fell asleep. This made it easy to take them in two stone chests to the Welsh mountain of Snowdon for burial. The red dragon later became one of the war symbols of the ancient Britons and Welsh, and today is one of the symbols of Wales.

Among Britain's other dragon legends are those in which the monster takes the form of a giant worm. England is rich in stories of such creatures. Of these the most renowned is the Lambton Worm, which was discovered by John de Lambton in the fast-flowing Wear River near his ancestral home in northeast England. It was a Sunday, and Lambton, the heir to the estate, should have been attending church. Instead he defiantly went fishing. It was not much fun for him when he hooked a great worm with nine holes on either side of its mouth. Foot by foot he dragged the huge, grotesque monster onto dry land, cursing the thing's size and ugliness. He thought he had caught "the Devil himself," and to get rid of it he threw it into a deep well nearby. He then went back home hoping that he had seen and heard the last of the worm. He shortly resumed his "God-defying" habit of Sunday fishing.

Some weeks later the worm reappeared. It crawled out of the well, coiled itself round a rock in the middle of the river, and lay there all day long. At night, however, it snaked ashore and pillaged the district. It attacked cattle, mangled cows and drank their milk, swallowed lambs in a single bite, and terrorized the local women and children. On witnessing this, and on seeing how the beast froze its victims on the spot with its "great big goggly eyes," Lambton confessed his responsibility for the worm's presence. In an attempt to lessen the monster's fury by good works, he joined one of the crusades to the Holy Land and was away for seven years. On his return to England, he learned from his father that the beast had increased its plunder. It uprooted trees in the area, killed all who tried to destroy it, and paid a daily visit to Lambton Hall to drink a large amount of milk it demanded as tribute. The heir to the estate determined to kill the worm, and visited a local sage, the so-called Wise Woman of Brugeford, to get advice on how to win the battle. "You will succeed," she told him, "but remember this. You must vow to kill the first being or person you meet as you recross the threshold of Lambton Hall. If you fail to do so, then none of the Lambtons for the next three-by-three generations will die in his bed."

Lambton agreed to the condition, put on a special suit of armor studded with blades, and went out to face his enemy. A desperate battle ensued. After an hour or more of savage fighting, in which the worm wound itself tightly around the knight's body, Lambton slew the monster. He then waded ashore and walked wearily to the Hall. Before entering the great manor he blew three notes on his bugle—a prearranged signal for the release of his hound Boris so that it would be the first to greet him as he entered. However, the plan misfired, and it was old Lord Lambton who reached the warrior before the rest. As the father started to embrace his son,

The Kiss That Conquered a Dragon

Once long ago a fiery dragon ate the two older sons of an emperor, whose youngest son went out to save them. This prince discovered that the dragon's great strength lay in a distant kingdom. There in a lake dwelled another dragon. Inside that dragon was a boar. Inside the boar was a hare. Inside the hare was a pigeon. Inside the pigeon was a sparrow. And inside the sparrow was the dragon's strength.

The brave young prince went to the faraway land and found the dragon. For two days they fought furiously, and each day the fight ended in a draw. During the fight the prince cried out: "If the princess would only kiss me on the forehead, I would throw you up to the sky!" This was reported to the emperor, who sent his daughter with the prince on the third day. The girl was deadly afraid, but she ran forward swiftly and kissed the prince on the forehead when he called for her. The prince then tossed the dragon high into the sky where it shattered into a hundred pieces. This freed the boar, the hare, the pigeon, and the sparrow in turn. The prince seized the first dragon's strength—but before he returned home to free his brothers, he married the beautiful princess.

the heir avoided him, called for Boris, and ran the hound through. But it was too late, for the vow had been broken. The Wise Woman's prediction came true, and the next nine generations of Lambton men died away from their beds. The first to die according to the prophecy was the monster-killer himself, who was slaughtered while on another crusade. The ninth Lambton to meet an unnatural death was Henry Lambton, Member of Parliament who represented the city of Durham. He was killed in June 1761 when his coach was in an accident on a bridge over the Wear River.

In China the dragons that stalked the land created no need for the country's heroes to kill them, eat their hearts, or drink their blood in order to become as strong, mighty, or keen-sighted. Dragons were regarded as benevolent rather than baleful. Far from gobbling up infants, violating virgins, and tangling with knights, they were gentle, charming creatures that brought hap-

Below left: in a German fairy tale a young couple decided to kill a dragon to gain his golden treasure for their marriage portion. They were both killed themselves—but, says the story, had the girl only known to tickle the dragon's chin, he would have purred contentedly while her lover safely took away the gold. Below: Fafnir, the fierce dragon of Norse and Germanic legend. He was once a man, but turned himself into a dragon in order to guard the treasure he had obtained by killing his father. The monster meets his death at the hands of a young hero with a magical sword.

piness and plenty. They could be found in rivers, lakes, and even —when they magically shrank themselves—in raindrops. Along with three other wholesome and well-intentioned creatures of legends—the tortoise, the phoenix, and the unicorn—they enjoyed lolling and basking in the sun. Occasionally they snacked on a swallow that flew into their jaws while pursuing flies. They were honored as the makers of humanitarian laws, and were held in particular esteem during the Ch'ing dynasty (1644–1912), when the emperors sat on dragon thrones, traveled by dragon boats, ate at dragon tables, and slept in dragon beds.

The Chinese affection for the beasts was made clear in this dictionary definition of around 1600, which stated: "The dragon is . . . the largest of scaled creatures. Its head is like a camel's, its horns like a deer's, its eyes like a hare's, its ears like a bull's, its neck like a snake's, its belly like a frog's, its scales like a carp's, its claws like an eagle's, and its paws like a tiger's. Its scales number

81, being nine by nine, the extreme odd and lucky number. Its voice is like the beating of a gong . . . When it breathes the breath forms clouds, sometimes changing into rain, at other times into fire . . . it is fond of beautiful gems and jade. It is extremely fond of swallow's flesh; it dreads iron, the *mong* plant, the centipede, the leaves of the Pride of India [the azedarac tree] and silk dyed in five different colors. When rain is wanted a swallow should be offered; when floods are to be restrained, then iron; to stir up the dragon the *mong* plant should be employed."

In spite of the help dragons gave, they were occasionally used for food and medicine. According to legend, a tasty soup was made of one particular dragon that fell into the palace grounds of the Emperor Hwo during a heavy shower around 100 B.C., and the hot liquid was served to the emperor's ministers. Dragons were also chopped into mincemeat and served at the tables of other emperors. In parts of China today pharmacies sell powdered and dried alligators, which are said to be descended from dragons, to cure anything from warts to lovesickness. However, even in the Far East the dragon was sometimes a malicious and predatory beast. Whenever upset or insulted, it could gather up all the neighborhood's water in containers and cause a drought. It could also turn on its old enemy the sun and cause an eclipse. The Japanese version of the monster often behaved more in keeping with the Western image. Some Japanese dragons demanded the sacrifice of a virgin once a year.

Legends from all over the world and, in particular, the legend of St. George and the dragon, once inspired a booming trade in fraudulent dragons and monsters throughout Europe. Imitation dragons were manufactured and sold as being straight from the caves and sandy banks of the Middle and Far East. The bogus monsters were displayed as early as the 16th century, when the renowned Italian physician and mathematician Hieronimus Cardanus saw some in Paris. "They were two-footed creatures with very small wings, which one could scarcely deem capable of flight, with a small head . . . like a serpent, of a bright color, and without any feather or hair," he recorded. The fake dragons were no larger than a kitten, so their sellers tried to pass them off as dragon babies. In fact, they were probably made by mutilating specimens of small flying lizards found in the Malay Peninsula and the East Indies. A scholar who examined one of the ugly specimens felt that all was not right. "Its head is serrated," he wrote, "and its crest comes to a peak . . . It has a flexible tail, two feet in length, and bristling with prickles. The skin is like that of a skate." Other false specimens were made by using parts of a giant ray fish, or by adding bat's wings to the dried-up body of a lizard.

Reports of dragons continued throughout the centuries, and many of them were included in various respected books. A 17th-century collection of fables, *Historie of Serpents*, told how dragons killed elephants by dropping on them from trees. In *The Subterranean World*, published in Amsterdam in 1678, the author Father Athanasius Kircher wrote that: "All the world's

Fig. X.

Reports of dragons in Europe were still current up to the 18th century. Left: a dragon was reportedly seen in a region of the Alps in 1660. Below: a sea dragon said to have been caught off the English coast in 1749 was four feet in length.

Sea Dragon

volcanoes are fed by one great main fire situated in the very bowels of the earth. Down in this area is a labyrinth of passageways, all running into each other, and most filled with lava, liquid fire, and water. Some of these caves and passageways, however, are empty, and it is here that you will find dragons, the kings of the underground beasts."

One of the most startling of dragon reports came from the small island of Komodo in the Malay Archipelago as recently as 1912. The pilot of a plane that crash-landed on Komodo afterward spoke of the "giant, lizard-like creatures" he had encountered. Although most people dismissed his story as "preposterous," the curator of the Botanical Gardens on Java decided to investigate the aviator's claims. He asked the Dutch Civil Administrator of the district to visit Komodo and see what he could find out. The administrator came back with the skin of a seven-foot-long creature, reporting that the local people swore there were similar beasts of up to 30 feet in length. On receipt of the skin and the information, the curator sent a Malay animal hunter to the island in search of a live monster. A local rajah provided special assistants and dogs. The hunt party captured four dragon-like animals, the biggest of them almost 10 feet long. They were later classified as belonging to a new species of giant monitor lizard, and are now known popularly as Komodo dragons.

In the summer of 1960 dragons again made the news. The place was New Guinea. The story was that local residents in an area of the island under Australian administration had been attacked by dragons some 20 feet long. Rumors flew that the monsters belched smoke and fire and sucked the blood from their victims' bodies. Some corpses also had wounds of more than a foot in length, said to have been made by the dragons' claws. There was so much panic that the government authorities moved people into police stockades, and posted a substantial reward for the capture of one of the beasts dead or alive. Perhaps not surprisingly, no one tried to collect the reward. Whether from boredom or over-feeding, the dragons themselves appeared no more.

The dragon is now considered by most people as a purely mythical beast. But its history and symbolism are so rich and diverse that the creature fascinates us more than many a real animal.

Below: a Komodo Dragon, a giant species of monitor lizard found on Komodo Island off the Malay peninsula. It is the closest thing to an actual dragon that has been scientifically reported. It first became known in 1912 when an airman made a forced landing on Komodo, and came back with tales of huge dragons that ate pigs and deer. Later investigation proved the existence of giant lizards on Komodo, of which at least one measured over nine feet.

2

Mermaids and Unicorns

On a warm summer day in the late 1890s William Munro, a teacher, was walking along the beach in the county of Caithness, Scotland. Suddenly he spotted a figure that resembled a naked woman seated on a rock jutting out to the sea. If he had not known that it was too dangerous to swim out to the rock, Munro would have assumed the figure to be human. But realizing that something was odd, he examined the figure closely. The lower part of the body was covered by water, but the creature was using her exposed arms to comb her long, light brown hair. After three or four minutes the figure dropped into the sea and vanished from view.

Unlike the fierce fire-breathing dragon, the seductive mermaid and the graceful unicorn breathe the eternal fragrance of a land of magical romance. Above: a unicorn drawn by the Swiss scientist Conrad Gesner in 1551. He speculated that the unicorn may have perished in the biblical great flood, and that bones found in Germany in his day might be unicorn horns washed there during the flood.

Right: the sheet music of an English variety show song popular in the 1860s. In this humorous ditty, at least one lonely sailor found a bride on the ocean floor.

24

MARRIED TO A MERMAID

SUNG BY

Mʳ ARTHUR LLOYD.

"She lures unresisting sailors to their doom"

As the result of an argument 12 years later, Munro wrote to *The Times* of London. In the published letter he described his earlier experience in careful and unemotional language. "The head was covered with hair of the color above mentioned [brown] and shaded on the crown, the forehead round, the face plump, the cheeks ruddy, the eyes blue, the mouth and lips of natural form resembling those of a man; the teeth I could not discover, as the mouth was shut; the breasts and abdomen, the arms and fingers of the size of a full-grown body of the human species, the fingers, from the action in which the hands were employed, did not appear to be webbed, but as to this I am not positive."

Munro went on to say that, although other reliable people had reported seeing the figure, he had not believed them until he had seen it himself. Having seen it, he was convinced that the figure was a mermaid. He finished by saying that he hoped his letter might help to establish "the existence of a phenomenon hitherto almost incredible to naturalists, or to remove the skepticism of others, who are ready to dispute everything they cannot comprehend . . . . "

This clear account shows that a belief in mermaids was not held only by half-crazed sailors on lengthy ocean voyages. In fact, the mermaid—like the dragon—seems to be a nearly universal symbol. She is found in most countries of the world, and where there is no sea, she adapts her home to a lake or river. Like the dragon, she seems to answer some deeply felt need in man. She is the unobtainable enchantress, seemingly sexual and voluptuous but underneath cold and elusive. With her eternal youth and beauty, her magical voice and seductive power, she lures unresisting sailors to their doom. She seems, in modern

Below: a German illustration of 1895 takes the erotic view of a mermaid ensnaring a human lover.

psychological interpretation, to symbolize the mingling of sex and death, the desire by man to lose himself totally even when he knows it means his own destruction.

Behind the mermaid legend lies a long sequence of romantic yearning, the longing for an ideal if unattainable woman whose favors were like those of no mere mortal. The very spot on which Munro had his "arresting experience" was the scene of an earlier and even more eventful happening. According to local stories a mermaid had given a young man gold, silver, and diamonds that she had gathered from a wrecked ship. The youth took her gifts but gave some of the jewels to young women he desired. Worse than this, he failed to meet the mermaid a number of times as planned, so arousing her jealousy and wrath. One day she met him in a boat and rowed him to a nearby cave, saying it held all the treasures ever lost in the estuary. Once there, the youth fell asleep. He awoke to find himself tied to a rock by gold chains that allowed him to walk only as far as a mound of diamonds at the mouth of the cave. Although he had riches and a mate who satisfied his lust, he was but a prisoner. He was trapped, a victim of his own greed.

Mermaids were well-known for taking ruthless revenge if thwarted or slighted in any way, and there are many stories that illustrate this characteristic. This theme may stem from man's sexual fantasy of a wild untameable creature bent on

Above: an illustration of the hero Odysseus, or Ulysses, and the sirens who lured men to their death by eerily beautiful singing, from the Greek epic poem by Homer. Although the poet did not describe the sirens physically, the early Greek artists usually portrayed them as part-woman, part-bird. Later, as in this version, they acquired the mermaid's tail. Odysseus resisted the sirens' songs by having himself lashed to the mast, and prevented his men from hearing them by plugging up their ears with beeswax.

Right: mermen are very rare, but this drawing is supposed to be of one seen with his mate in the Nile in ancient times. It appeared in a book by the Italian naturalist Ulysses Aldrovandi in 1599. In an 18th-century account of the event, it was said that the creatures remained in full view of several people for at least two hours.

Right: a magnificant French 16th-century pendant of pearls and rubies in the shape of a merman. By logical development of the many factual and mythical tales of treasure ships sinking to the bottom of the sea, mermaids came frequently to be associated with fabulously rich hoards of jewels and great heaps of bright gold.

fulfilling her own desires. Even more sinister in terms of sexual symbolism is the idea of the mermaid as a fallen angel who could only eat living flesh. She captured sailors by her singing and sweet music. If this technique failed—which it rarely did—she relied on a unique body smell that no man could resist. Once she had snared her victim, and lulled him to sleep, she tore him to pieces with her spiky green teeth.

Slightly less savage as a fantasy was the myth that mermaids and mermen lived in a kingdom of great riches beneath the sea to which mermaids took their victims and kept them prisoner. From this tale grew the seaman's belief that it means bad luck to see a mermaid. It was supposed to foretell death at sea by drowning.

The roots of the mermaid legend go back to the powerful Babylonian fish deities associated with the sun and the moon. Oannes, who represented the sun, had a human form but wore a fish head as a cap and a fish skin as a cloak. He was gradually replaced by the fish god Ea who was half man and half fish, and can be seen as the ancestor of the merman. The moon goddess Atargartis, half woman and half fish, was the precursor of the mermaid. The Babylonians believed that when they had finished their respective journeys through the sky, the sun and moon sank into the sea. So it seemed appropriate that the gods of the sun and moon should have a form that allowed for life both above and below the water. The strange form of these gods, part human and part fish, and their power to vanish into the unfathomable oceans gives them a mysterious, elusive quality. This mystery and elusiveness was inherited by mermaids. The mirror the mermaid often holds is thought to represent the moon, which also seems to add to her power because of the way the moon influences the tides. Because the fish deities were accorded enormous power in pre-Christian times, their link to the mermaids helped strengthen the mermaid legends.

Other forerunners of the mermaids were the tritons of Greek mythology. Also half human and half fish, the tritons calmed the waves and ruled the storms. The sirens of Greek mythology, although half bird and half woman, like the mermaid lured men to destruction by their beautiful singing. When the Greek hero Ulysses was forced to sail past them, he plugged the ears of his sailors with wax, and had himself bound securely to the mast in order to be able to resist them.

The Apsaras of India were beautiful water nymphs, but despite their human shape, they had much in common with mermaids. Besides their beauty and "fragrance," they were skilled musicians, especially on the lute, and shared the mermaid's power of prophecy. However, though promiscuous and always eager for new conquests, they were friendly toward man, and intent on giving happiness.

With the establishment of Christianity, the mermaid legend took on a new aspect in which the mermaid longed to have a soul. According to Christian thought, the mermaid could only gain a soul by promising to live on land and giving up all hope of returning to the sea. This was impossible for the half-fish creature, so it doomed her to an unhappy struggle with herself.

Above: in ancient Hindu sculpture the important god Vishnu is seen as a semi-fish. In the story of how Vishnu saved humankind during his first incarnation, the god appeared "on the vast ocean in the form of a fish, blazing with gold."

240. Monstre semblable à une **Sirenne** pris à la côte de l'isle de **Borné** ou **Boeren** dans le Departement d'Amboi
Il étoit long de 39. pouces gros à proportion comme une Anguille. Il a vécu à terre dans une Cuve pleine d'eau quatre
jours et sept heures. Il poussoit de temps en temps des petits cris comme ceux d'une Souris. Il ne voulut point manger.
quoy qu'on luy offrit des petits poissons, des coquillages, des Crabes, Ecrevisses, etc. On trouva dans sa Cuve apres qu'il
fut mort quelques excrements semblables à des crottes de chat.

Above: the mermaid of Amboina, caught on the coast of Borneo, was reported to have lived for over four days after capture. This picture was said to have been "drawn from life," and was published in an elegant volume—lavishly illustrated—published by Louis Renard in Amsterdam in 1717. The drawings were made by Samuel Fallours from specimens in the collection of the governor-regent of the province of Amboina.

Thus the mermaid, who had been a simple figure representing the most elemental urges and desires, became far more complex, with her own internal conflicts. There is a sad and charming story of a mermaid in the 6th century A.D. who daily visited a monk in the holy community of Iona, a small island off Scotland. She begged to be given a soul, and the monk prayed with her to give her the strength to abandon the sea. But despite her desire for a soul, and despite the fact that she had fallen passionately in love with the monk, she was unable to give up the sea. In the end, weeping bitterly, she left the island forever. It is said that the tears she shed became pebbles, and to this day, the gray-green pebbles found on the shore of Iona are known as mermaid's tears.

The seal, with its sleek form and human characteristics, has long been linked with the mermaid. Many believe that reports of mythical mermaids are based on glimpses of real seals. In mermaid lore, however, the seal is known as the constant companion of the mermaid. There is a story that a fisherman once stunned and skinned a seal, and then threw it back live into the sea. A mermaid, taking pity on the animal, volunteered to search for its skin. However, she was captured by the fisherman's companions and died from exposure to the air. Ever since then, in gratitude for her bravery, the seal has been the special guardian of the mermaid.

The Scandinavians, Scots, and Irish had many stories about seal people who were forced to live as seals at sea, but who could at certain times assume their true human shape on land. Some thought seals were fallen angels, others that they were the souls of drowned people or humans under a spell. Certain Irish families claimed descent from seals, and an entire nation in Asia Minor traced their ancestry back to a seal maiden

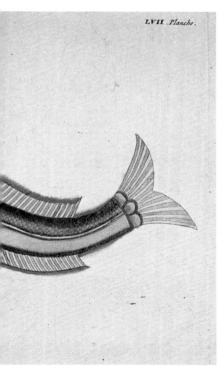

mentioned in Greek mythology. In the myth a water nymph transformed herself into a seal to evade the unwelcome attentions of the son of Zeus. However, her precautions were too late, for soon after her transformation she gave birth to a son. He was named Phocus, which means seal. The Phocian people commemorated their descendance from the seal maiden by showing a seal on their earliest coins.

Seal maidens had much in common with mermaids, and the two creatures became inextricably mixed in many legends. Mermaids and seal maidens both liked to dance and sing. They also both shared the gift of prophecy. There are stories of both seal maidens and mermaids marrying humans and remaining on land for many years. It was said that a mermaid had an enchanted cap without which she could not return to sea. If a man managed to steal her cap and hide it, he might marry her; but if she ever found it she would immediately vanish into the waves. In the same way a man could marry a seal maiden if he could steal and hide her sealskin. An old story from the Scottish highlands is one of many on this theme. A man fell in love with a beautiful seal maiden, stole her sealskin and hid it carefully, and married her. They had many children and were happy. But one day one of her sons discovered where the skin was hidden and told his mother. She

Right: in the last century the Japanese made skillful mermaid fakes with torsos of monkeys and tails of fish—but they were far from the beauties of the myths. Below: another unattractive fake mermaid of the type exhibited by P. T. Barnum in the 1870s. He fooled the public with pictures of lovely mermaids outside the tent.

eagerly put it on and, leaving her children forever, swam joyfully out to sea.

In 1403 a mermaid reportedly floated through a broken dyke near Edam in Holland, and was taken into captivity. Her fate was different from most other captured mermaids. She spent the next 15 years in Haarlem where she was taught to spin and to obey her mistress. On death she was given a Christian burial.

In some areas mermaid legend survived a long time. As recently as 1895 the inhabitants of the Welsh seaport of Milford Haven believed that mermaids or underwater fairies regularly shopped at the town's weekly market. They got to the town by means of a covered road on the sea bed, quietly made their purchases, such as tortoiseshell combs for their hair, and vanished till next market day.

Most sightings of mermaids, however, have been by sailors. For instance, during his first voyage, the previously skeptical Christopher Columbus recorded seeing three mermaids leaping high out of the sea off the coast of Guiana. Mermaids were regularly seen by sailors suffering from months of boredom and sexual frustration at sea. Could sexual fantasizing have made them see a beautiful half-woman in sea mammals such as graceful seals, or even ungainly dugongs or manatees? Who knows?

The famous English navigator Henry Hudson told his mermaid story matter of factly. On June 15, 1625, while sailing in search of the North West Passage, he wrote in his diary: "One of our company, looking overboard, saw a mermaid. From the navel upward, her back and breasts were like a woman's . . . her skin very white, and long hair hanging down behind, of color black. In her going down they saw her tail, which was like the tail of a porpoise, speckled like a mackerel." There are reports of sightings from Russia—where the mermaids were "tall, sad, and pale"—from Thailand, and from Scotland. In the last country in May 1658 mermaids were found at the mouth of the River Dee and the *Aberdeen Almanac* promised visitors that they "will undoubtedly see a pretty Company of Mermaids, creatures of admirable beauty."

Pesce-Dona ou poisson femme sur le ventre.

Right: an 18th-century French engraving showing two views of a manatee seen in the Congo River. It was called a "woman fish." Below: the manatee under water. It is hardly a tribute to women that men—even womenless men—saw this cumbrous animal as a mermaid.

Perce-Dona ou poisson femme sur le dos

As the fame of mermaids spread, so the inevitable fakes and frauds began to appear. Usually false mermaids were carefully constructed from the top half of a monkey joined to the tail of a fish. One of these, probably made in the 17th century, was shown in an exhibition of fakes mounted by the British Museum in London in 1961. Most of these so-called mermaids were extremely ugly, but they seemed to have aroused great interest.

In a book published in 1717 there is a picture of a supposedly genuine mermaid. The description with the picture said: "A monster resembling a Siren caught on the coast of Borneo in the administrative district of Amboina. It was 59 inches long and in proportion like an eel. It lived on land for four days and seven hours in a barrel filled with water. From time to time it uttered little cries like those of a mouse. Although offered small fish, molluscs, crabs, crayfish, etc., it would not eat . . . . "

As the fame of this mermaid spread, Peter the Great, Czar of Russia, got interested and tried to get more information from François Valentijn, a Dutch colonial chaplain who had written on the subject. Valentijn didn't add much but reported on another Amboina mermaid. This time the creature was accompanied by her mate, and was seen by more than 50 witnesses. The writer was convinced that the mermaid story was true. "If any narrative in the world deserves credit," he wrote, "it is this . . . Should the stubborn world, however, hesitate to believe it, it matters nothing; for there are people who would even deny the existence of such cities as Rome, Constantinople, or Cairo, simply because they themselves have not happened to see them."

Despite the fact that mermaids were supposed to be wanton and cruel they were sought after by seamen as if they were virginal and kind. Such was the enthusiasm to find a mermaid—and then presumably keep her for private pleasure—that the ships' lookouts began to see the heroine of their erotic dreams everywhere. As one writer later put it, "These hauntingly beautiful goddesses of the sea, full of mystery and danger, were surely conjured from the chaos of the water in answer to some primal human need." But the great 18th-century German naturalist, G. W. Steller, seemed to have a rather different image of the origin of mermaids. Up to the time that he joined an expedition seeking a sea route from Siberia to Alaska, sightings of mermaids had been dismissed by some experts as being distorted glimpses of the dugong or manatee. Such water mammals suckled their young and, ran the explanation, a sight of mother mammal suckling her baby gave rise to tales about beautiful sea maidens with shapely naked breasts.

On the expedition's return voyage, Steller's ship was wrecked. He and others were washed up on Copper Island in the Commander Group near Bering Island. It was there at high tide that Steller saw some "hump-backed" objects in the water. At first they reminded him of capsized boats. On seeing them again, however, he realized that they were seal-like animals of a previously unknown class. He gave them the name of *Rhytina stelleri,* or Steller's sea-cow, and claimed that it was these somewhat unfortunately named creatures that had for so long been taken for mermaids. He was the first trained observer

Above: mermaids and wild men together in a 15th-century French coat-of-arms. Mermaids became a favorite heraldic emblem early, and the graceful maids from the sea rode into battle on countless banners.

Right: perhaps it was the dream of every fisherman to take as his catch the fabled creature with the body of a voluptous woman.

to have seen this animal alive. He estimated that they were an average of 30 feet long and weighed some $3\frac{1}{2}$ tons each. They had small heads and large forked tails. Subsequent investigation proved that they mated like human beings—especially in the spring on evenings when the sea was calm.

"Before they come together," he wrote, "many amorous preludes take place. The female, constantly followed by the male, swims leisurely to and fro, eluding him with many gyrations and meanderings until, impatient of further delay, she turns on her back as if exhausted and coerced, whereupon the male, rushing violently upon her, pays her the tribute of his passion, and both give themselves over in mutual embrace."

Throughout the Middle Ages carvings and stone and wooden representations of mermaids adorned churches and cathedrals in almost every part of Europe. But by the middle of the more scientific 19th century, belief in them was ebbing. As steamships replaced sailing ships and the duration of voyages grew shorter, seamen less and less claimed to have been seduced, tempted, or taunted by the lethal sirens. In spite of this, the mermaid had not yet completely submerged. One was seen again in 1900 by Alexander Gunn, a landholder in the far north of Scotland. While he and his dog were out rescuing a sheep that had become stuck in a gully, he glanced up and locked eyes with a mermaid reclining on an adjacent ledge. With red-gold wavy hair, green eyes, and arched eyebrows she was extremely beautiful. She was also of human size. It was hard to tell who was the more startled—she, Gunn, or his dog. However, it was the dog which, with a terrified howl, gave vent to its feelings

34

first. It fled with its tail between its legs, followed close behind by the landholder who had seen anger as well as fear in the mermaid's expression. "What I saw was real," he told a friend later. "I actually encountered a mermaid."

More than 50 years later, two girls sauntering along the same shore also chanced upon a mermaid stranded by the tide. Her description fitted that of Gunn's. Shortly after this, in a completely different part of the world, the adventurer Eric de Bisschop added to the relatively few 20th-century accounts of mermaids. His experiences occurred shortly after midnight on January 3, 1957, when he was sailing his reconstruction of an ancient Polynesian raft from Tahiti to Chile. In his book, *Tahiti-Nui*, published two years later, he told how one of the sailors on watch suddenly began to act like he had gone mad. The man claimed he had seen a strange creature leap out of the water and onto the deck. The being, with hair like extremely fine seaweed, stood upright on its tail. The sailor approached and touched the intruder, which immediately knocked him flat and then jumped into the sea. It was the shining fish scales on the seaman's arms that convinced de Bisschop the man was telling

The Little Mermaid and the Sea Witch

Hans Christian Andersen's little mermaid was the most beautiful of the Sea King's six daughters. She longed for a life on land and an immortal soul. When she saw the handsome young prince and learned that if she gained the love of a mortal she could have a soul that would live forever, she determined to do so — even though the Sea Witch warned her that the price of failure was instant death. The Sea Witch changed her fishtail into legs, but every step hurt her as if she were treading on a sharp-edged knife. In return for the charm, the Sea Witch demanded the mermaid's tongue, and she became mute.

The prince found the exquisite speechless girl and lovingly took care of her, but he did not think of taking her as his wife. At length he met a beautiful princess and married her. The mermaid's sisters appeared and told the little mermaid that if she plunged a knife in the prince's heart she could still be saved. The little mermaid refused, and for this act of mercy she was swept into the skies to become one of the Air Spirits, who after 300 years of good deeds are rewarded with a soul and go to heaven.

LA GIRAUDIERE

the truth, and that he had been in contact with a mermaid. Four years later, in 1961, the Isle of Man Tourist Board introduced an angling week and offered a prize to anyone catching a live mermaid in the Irish Sea. This followed several reports of red-headed water nymphs sporting in the foam. However, the Gaelic mermaids proved as elusive as their sisters of centuries before, and none was caught.

Though there are probably only a few people today who would genuinely subscribe to a belief in real mermaids, it might be said that mermaids have attained a degree of reality. The legend is so powerful and universal that, like the dragon, the mermaid has become a symbol—part of man's unconscious imagination. The same can be said for the unicorn.

This mythical creature is based on a variety of animals, but is always distinguished from others by its long single horn. Like the dragon, its general appearance and characteristics varied according to place and legend. Sometimes it strongly resembled one animal such as a goat, a horse, or even a serpent, and sometimes it combined the features of different animals. In the West it tended to be fierce and untameable, a lover of solitude, but in China it was peaceful and gentle and heralded good fortune.

Like other mythical beasts the unicorn provides a rich field for symbolic interpretation, both of a specific and of a generalized kind. The single horn indicates both virility and kingly power, and is also, in some legends, a sign of purity. The unicorn combines both male and female elements with its masculine horn and female body. Its Chinese name, ki-lin means male-female. This reconciliation of the opposing forces of male and female in one creature meant, in symbolic terms, that the

Left: the last panel of *The Hunt of the Unicorn* shows the mythical creature in captivity. The theme of the unicorn and the hunt was a favorite of artists throughout the Middle Ages. They were drawn by the grace of the animal and the richness of the complex symbolism surrounding the whole legend.

Right: the part of the old French tapestry showing the unicorn in the lap of a virgin. She will fondle him until he falls asleep; then the huntsmen will take him. Modern psychology puts a strong sexual interpretation on this unicorn legend, but many earlier Christians saw it as an allegory of the incarnation of Christ.

unicorn stood for the reconciliation of other opposites. The harmony of opposites was the greatest ideal of Western magicians and alchemists, and the unicorn therefore has an important place in the history of magic.

The first mention of the unicorn in the West was in a book on India written by the Greek historian Ctesias in about 398 B.C. Part of his description went: "There are in India certain wild asses which are as large as horses, and larger. Their bodies are white, their heads dark red, and their eyes dark blue. They have a horn on the forehead which is about a foot and a half in length." The description seems to be based on conjecture and travelers' tales. The unicorn appears to be a mixture of the rhinoceros, the Himalayan antelope, and the wild ass. Its horn was said to have come to a long sharp point, and to be white at the base, black in the center, and crimson at the tip. It is probable that Ctesias had seen drinking cups made of horn and decorated in these colors inasmuch as such drinking horns were often used by Indian princes. He reports that dust scraped from the horn was an antidote to poison, and that those who drank from the horn would be protected from convulsions and from poisoning. This belief persisted up to the Middle Ages, and the rich and powerful paid enormous prices for drinking vessels believed to be made from the horn of the unicorn.

Apothecaries often claimed to keep a unicorn's horn in their shop in order to cure ailments. Some even thought it had the

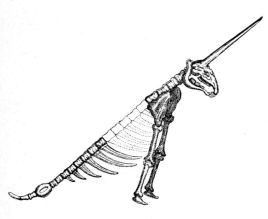

Above: a unicorn skeleton reconstructed from fossil bones in 1749. By that time, scientists were more skeptical about unicorns. Then, in the next century, a leading naturalist declared that a single-horned animal with a cloven hoof was genetically impossible. With that, the graceful unicorn finally withdrew into the mists of legend and myth.

Below: the British royal coat-of-arms. When James VI of Scotland became James I of England in 1603, he added the unicorn as a heraldic emblem. This mythical animal had long been one of the royal beasts of Scottish rulers.

power to raise the dead. Even in the 17th and 18th centuries alicorn, a powder allegedly made from unicorn horn, was featured on the drug lists issued by the English Royal Society of Physicians. It was extremely expensive, and gave rise to the saying "weight for weight alicorn for gold." The druggists explained the high costs by the fact that unicorns were mostly caught in India, and that the powder had to be shipped from there.

In 1641 a French marquis visiting London wrote that he had seen a unicorn's horn on display in the Tower of London. It had been the property of Queen Elizabeth I, and was said to have then been worth about £40,000. He wanted to test its authenticity by placing it on a piece of silk and putting both articles on a hot coal fire. If the horn was genuine, he said, the silk would not burn. However, perhaps fortunately, the presence of the guards prevented him from carrying out this test.

The purifying nature of the unicorn's horn is apparent in a famous medieval legend. In this story many animals gather at dusk by a pool to quench their thirst, but the water is poisoned and they are unable to drink. Soon they are joined by the unicorn who dips his horn into the water and cleanses it. In some Christian versions, the horn stands for the cross and the water for the sins of the world.

Another famous and symbolic medieval legend is the capture of the unicorn by a young virgin. The unicorn, a small goat-like creature, was too fierce and swift to be captured by hunters. It could only be tamed by a virgin seated alone in a forest under a tree. Attracted by her perfume of chastity, the unicorn would approach and lay its head in her lap. She would stroke its horn and lull it to sleep. Then she would cut off his horn and betray him to the hunters and dogs. The sexual symbolism of this story is fairly obvious, and it gave rise to many erotic elaborations. There was also an attempt to put a Christian interpretation on it. In this case the virgin is the Virgin Mary, the unicorn is Christ, and the horn signifies the unity of father and son. Christ, as embodied in the unicorn, is slain for the sake of a sinful world.

For centuries naturalists suggested that it should be possible to produce a unicorn by genetic engineering, and in March 1933 it was done. An American biologist, Dr. Franklin Dove, performed a simple operation on a day-old male Ayrshire calf at the University of Maine. By transplanting the animal's two horn buds and placing them together over the frontal bones, he forecast that a single unicorn-like horn would grow. His experiment was a total success and he was able to show the world a one-horned bull. It was nothing like the unicorn of the Middle Ages, which through courtly literature had gradually assumed the sleek lines of a horse. But it was not bullish in character. Could people centuries ago have performed the same experiment and produced a one-horned creature, with characteristics that differed from its two-horned brethren? And could these creatures have inspired the original legends of the unicorn? Or did the unicorn, a mysterious and magical creature, spring purely from man's mind, meeting some psychological and imaginative need?

Right: an advertisement for unicorn's horn—usually called alicorn—which throughout the Middle Ages was considered a powerful antidote against poison. It was also supposed to be a cure for the plague and other diseases. A unicorn's horn purified water, and a drinking cup made of this horn guaranteed that any poison placed in it would be rendered harmless—an obvious asset for insecure monarchs of the day. The powdered form was the easiest way to take alicorn internally, but avaricious pharmacists produced "unicorn water" merely by standing one end of the horn in water, as in this 17th-century illustration.

Below: the one-horned rhinoceros, almost certainly one of the main sources for the unicorn myth. Even at the height of belief in the unicorn, learned men were aware of the existence of the rhinoceros, and certain that it was definitely distinct from the unicorn—although this did not prevent them from confusing rhinoceros and unicorn attributes.

UNICORNS HORN

Now brought in Use for the Cure of Diseases by an Experienced DOCTOR, the AUTHOR of this Antidote.

A Most Excellent Drink made with a true *Unicorns Horn*, which doth Effectually Cure these Diseases:

Further, If any please to be satisfied, they may come to the Doctor and view the *Horn.*

viz.
- Scurvy, Old Ulcers,
- Dropsie,
- Running Gout,
- Consumptions, Distillations, Coughs
- Palpitation of the Heart,
- Fainting Fits, Convulsions,
- Kings Evil, Rickets in Children,
- Melancholly or Sadness,
- The Green Sickness, Obstructions,

And all Distempers proceeding from a Cold Cause.

The Use of it is so profitable, that it prevents Diseases and Infection by fortifying the Noble Parts, and powerfully expels what is an Enemy to Nature, preserving the Vigour, Youth, and a good Complexion to Old Age: The Virtue is of such force, as to resist an Injury from an unsound Bedfellow; None can excel this, for it is joyned with the Virtue of a true *Unicorns Horn*, through which the Drink passeth, and being impregnated therewith, it doth wonderfully Corroborate and Cure, drinking it warm at any time of the Day, about a quarter of a Pint at a time, the oftner the better, the Price is 2 s. the Quart.

2. Also as a preparative for this excellent Drink, and good against the Diseases above mentioned, and all Crudities in the Body, is ready prepared twelve Pils in a Box to be taken at three Doses, according to Directions therewith given, the Price is 2 s. the Box.

3. Likewise he hath Admirable Medicines for the Cure of the POX, or Running of the Reins, with all Simptoms and Accidents thereto belonging, whether Newly taken or of long Continuance, and (by God's Blessing) secures the Patient from the danger of the Disease presently, and perfects the Cure with the greatest Speed and Secresie imaginable, not hindering Occasions, or going abroad: Whosoever makes Use of these Admirable Medicines, may have further Advice from the Doctor without Charge.

The Doctor Liveth in Hounsditch, *next Door to* Gun-Yard, *have-*

Monsters
of the Deep

In 1938 a strange fish was picked up in the nets of a South African trawler. It turned out to be a coelacanth, a fish that had been in existence about 300 million years ago, and was believed by scientists to have been extinct for about 70 million years. The coelacanth had no special protective features, so its survival all these millions of years was particularly remarkable. If the lowly coelacanth had such powers to survive, why not other ancient marine species? Might there be a few survivors somewhere in the depths of the ocean? The sea is vast and incredibly deep. Ships travel over only a small portion of the surface, and trawlers

The oceans, so full of unknown possibilities, have fascinated generations of sailors passing over their surface, and also land-dwellers staring out over the apparently empty expanses. In such vastness, surely anything might live? In such unimaginable depths, surely some terrible gigantic creature might find a cold, silent, but safe refuge? Right: a mermaid and a sea serpent leap out of their watery element on the cover of a German magazine published in 1897.

"Suddenly, a giant sea monster emerged"

Below: this illustration for a Jules Verne story shows a giant squid "brandishing the victim like a feather." Do the huge and terrifying sea monsters of fiction have real-life counterparts? That is still an unanswered question.

normally sink their nets to a depth of about 60 feet. Until recently scientists believed that fish could not survive at great depths, but a research vessel has now brought up a fish from a depth of over 26,000 feet. Although the ocean at that level is totally black, that fish still retained two small eyes—evidence that it had once lived far closer to the surface. We know that marine creatures are amazingly adaptable. Salmon leap rapids. A variety of lung fish can live out of water for four years. It is not impossible that certain prehistoric sea monsters have adapted to living in the ocean deeps.

At one time, perhaps as long as 200 million years ago, the sea was filled with giant monsters. There were massive sharks far larger than any we know today, enormous crabs, sea serpents of fantastic lengths, and huge lung fish, skates, and rays. Many of these creatures developed body armor and protective devices such as stings to insure their survival. In 1930 Dr. Anton Brun caught the six-foot-long larva of an eel at a depth of only 1000 feet. On the assumption that it would mature to 18 times its length—although some eels reach 30 times their larval size—this eel would grow to a mammoth 110 feet. Perhaps there are still larger species existing at still greater depths.

But whether they exist or not, sea monsters have long been a part of mariners' tales. Among the many stories is one that took place in the late 18th century when a Danish sailing ship had been becalmed off the coast of West Africa. Her captain, Jean-Magnus Dens, decided to put the time to good use and ordered the crew to scrape and clean the outside of the boat. To do this the men worked from planks on the ship's side. Suddenly, without warning, a giant sea monster emerged. Wrapping two of its enormous arms around two of the men, it dragged them into the sea. A third arm went around another sailor, but, as he clung desperately to the rigging, his shipmates freed him by hacking off the monster's arm. Despite repeated attempts to harpoon the monster, it sank out of sight into the water. The bodies of the first two victims were never recovered, and the third sailor died that same night. The captain later described the part of the arm that had been hacked off. He said it was very thick at one end and tapered to a sharp point at the other. It was about 25 feet long and covered with large suckers. Judging from the size of the cut-off portion, the captain estimated that the whole arm must have been between 35 to 40 feet in length.

This is a typical seaman's story of a monstrous sea creature—exaggerated, fantastical, but fascinating. Such stories were often believed in earlier times. However, even in the late 18th century, Captain Dens could find few to credit his. The big exception was the young French naturalist Pierre Denys de Montfort, who was determined to prove to the skeptical scientific world that octopuses of collosal size existed. Choosing to believe that Dens' monster was a huge octopus, he included Dens' account in his unfinished six-volume work *The Natural History of Molluscs*. These books were published in Paris between 1802 and 1805, and, unfortunately for Denys de Montfort's reputation, he included a mixture of science and imagination in which fact was hard to distinguish from fiction. The Frenchman's one

Above: a painting said to have been presented to a church by the grateful crew that escaped death at the hands of the monster shown. The original had been lost, but French naturalist Pierre Denys de Montfort had another painted from word-of-mouth description because he felt it was proof of the existence of monstrous sea creatures.

Left: the capture of a giant squid by the French gunboat *Alecton* on November 30, 1861. Attracted by a huge, mysterious floating mass off Tenerife, the commander, Lieutenant Bouyer, went over to investigate. He discovered an oversized squid between 15 and 18 feet long with arms of five to size feet. The men succeeded in harpooning it, but when they tried to haul it ashore the body broke, and they recovered only the end of the tail. Although the fragment looked and smelled like animal matter, French scientists concluded that it was probably a piece of seaweed.

Above: a 19th-century woodcut of a kraken—legendary Norwegian sea monster—attacking a sailing ship. It has been speculated that the silent sailing ships, gliding across the surface as they did, were far more likely to encounter sea creatures than noisy engine-driven craft, which create warning vibrations in the water for considerable distances. Below: an artist's impression of the gigantic squid caught off the coast of Newfoundland in 1878, shown with a man next to it to indicate scale. The body was 20 feet long, and one of the arms alone was 35 feet. It is the biggest specimen accepted by science as a genuine giant sea animal.

scientific supporter was the German naturalist Lorenz Oken, who, for all his renown, was slightly suspect because he also believed there were more and stranger things beneath the surface of the sea than had ever been seen above it. Despite great ridicule and criticism, Denys de Montfort continued to compile reports of "the sightings of monsters and serpents of the sea by mariners whose sincerity I do not and will not doubt."

True to his word, he followed every lead to find his giant octopus. Sometime in the 1790s he journeyed to the northern port of Dunkirk, where a group of American whale fishers were living and working. He wanted to interview the seamen and hear at first hand of the experiences that few people apart from himself would credit. For example, here is a report he repeated: "One of these captains, named Ben Johnson, told me that he had harpooned a male whale, which, besides its very prominent penis placed under the belly, seemed to have another one coming out of its mouth. This surprised him greatly, and also the sailors, and when they had made the whale fast to the ship,

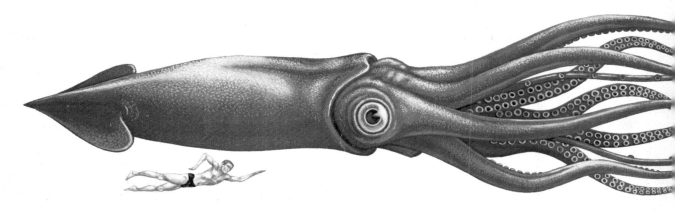

46

he had them put a hook through this long round mass of flesh which they hauled in with several running nooses . . . They could hardly believe their eyes when they saw that this fleshy mass, cut off at both ends and as thick as a mast at the widest point, was the arm of an enormous octopus, the closed suckers of which were larger than a hat; the lower end seemed newly cut off, the upper one . . . was also cut off and scarred and surmounted by a sort of extension as thick and long as a man's arm. This huge octopus's limb, exactly measured with a fishing line, was found to be 35 feet long, and the suckers were arranged in two rows, as in the common octopus. What then must have been the length of arm which had been cut off at its upper extremity where it was no less than six inches in diameter?" It seemed to Denys de Montfort that at least 10 feet had been sliced off the upper end, and a further 10 to 25 feet off the lower—making a total length of some 80 feet.

During his stay in Dunkirk, he found that the whale fishers were eager to speak of their encounters with monsters. He gave an account of what was told by an American captain named Reynolds. "One day," Denys de Montfort recorded, "he and his men saw floating on the surface of the water a long fleshy body, red and slate colored, which they took to be a sea serpent, and which frightened the sailors who rowed the whaleboats." However one sailor noticed that the supposed snake had no head and was motionless, so they found the courage to haul it aboard. They then discovered from the suckers that it was an octopus or squid arm—one that measured 45 feet in length and $2\frac{1}{2}$ feet in diameter.

The arm, which would have been a convincing piece of evidence, was nowhere to be found by the time Denys de Montfort heard about it. Although disappointed at not seeing it, the naturalist's hopes rose when he heard of an extraordinary painting of a sea monster on view further along the coast in St. Malo. He hurried to go to St. Thomas's chapel where the picture, given in thanksgiving for their survival by a ship's crew, was hanging. Before inspecting it, however, he quizzed several of the port's fishermen about its story. They related how a local sailing ship had run into trouble off the West African coast, and how her crew had been set upon by a "monster straight from Hell." As Denys de Montfort told it from the accounts he heard:

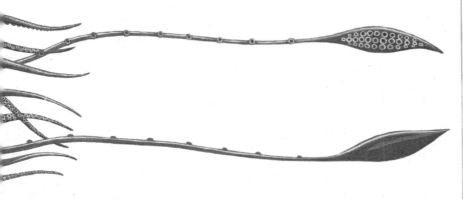

The Monster from the Sea

Late in the 18th century a sailing ship off the coast of West Africa found itself becalmed in a placid ocean. The wind had dropped, and Jean-Magnus Dens, the Danish captain, ordered his crew to lower planks off the side from which they could scrape and clean the ship. Three men climbed onto the planks and began their work. They were scraping energetically when suddenly, out of the quiet sea around them, rose an immense octopus or squid. It seized two of the men and pulled them under the water. The third man leaped desperately into the rigging, but a gigantic arm pursued him, getting caught up in the shrouds. The sailor fainted from shock, and his horrified shipmates frantically hacked at the great tentacle, finally chopping it off. Meanwhile, five harpoons were being driven into the body of the beast in the forlorn hope of saving the two who had disappeared. The frightful struggle went on until, one by one, four of the lines broke. The men had to give up the attempt at killing the monster, which sank out of view.

The unconscious sailor, hanging limply in the shrouds, was gently taken down and placed in his bunk. He revived a little, but died in raving madness that night.

Right: a decorated Greek vase showing the struggle of the hero Heracles with the river-god Achelous to win Deianeira. The god is represented with a man's torso atop a sea serpent's body. The Greeks usually depicted river-gods with beards and horns, the latter being a symbol of power.

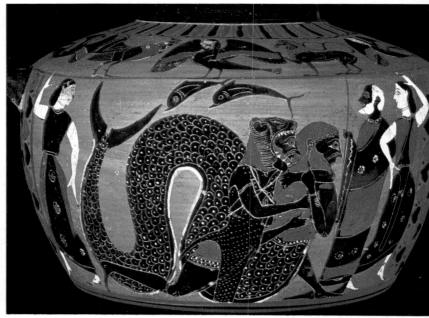

Above: a sea monster described by Olaus Magnus and illustrated in his book published in 1555. His sea monster is a long serpent-like creature with a head about the size of a man. Olaus Magnus felt that the appearance of a creature like this was a portent of change, probably for the worse.

Above: the legendary sea monk of 16th-century Norway. It was said to have a head like a monk's cowl, a human face, and a fishtail.

"The ship had just taken in her cargo of slaves, ivory, and gold dust, and the men were heaving up anchor, when suddenly a monstrous cuttlefish appeared on top of the water and slung its arms about two of the masts. The tips of the arms reached to the mastheads, and the weight of the cuttle dragged the ship over, so that she lay on her beam-ends and was near to being capsized. The crew seized axes and knives, and cut away at the arms of the monster; but, despairing of escape, called upon their patron saint, St. Thomas, to help them. Their prayers seemed to give them renewed courage, for they persevered, and finally succeeded in cutting off the arms, when the animal sank and the vessel was righted. Now, when the ship returned to St. Malo the crew, grateful for their deliverance from so hideous a danger, marched in procession to the chapel of their patron saint, where they offered a solemn thanksgiving, and afterwards had a painting made representing the conflict with the cuttle, and which was hung in the chapel."

On hearing this story, Denys de Montfort rushed into the chapel as eagerly as the seamen themselves had done, and gazed up at the fantastic and fearsome scene that the painting depicted. The monster, whose arms were wound around the tops of the three masts, was as gigantic and hideous as the naturalist could have yearned for, and he was grateful for the boost it gave to his theories. He took the painting to be an exact description of a real event, which his obsessional belief in monstrous octopuses made entirely plausible to him. He had a copy of the painting made by an artist who had not seen the original, and who therefore made it seem even more fantastic. On publication of the copy, critics called it an even bigger fake than his books. He was branded "the most outrageous charlatan Paris has known," and no one accepted his challenge to travel the 200 miles to St. Malo to see the original for themselves. The picture was later taken from the chapel and either hidden or destroyed. Denys de Montfort sank into disrepute and obscurity. He wrote a phrase book and a book on bee-keeping, and, on their failure, became a pedlar of sea shells. Having fallen into deep poverty, he was found dead in a gutter in 1820 or 1821. His reputation as an eccentric overshadowed his fine early work on mollusc shells, and it was too soon forgotten that he had created 25 new genera still in use today.

For some decades after, no naturalists were prepared to risk their career by writing about marine monsters, whether or not they thought some of the tales might have a basis in fact. A more recent author views the whole subject in more perspective, however, and writes: "The sea serpent—or at any rate his cousin, the sea monster . . . is at least as ancient, and therefore as respectable, as the fairies, and a good deal older than the modern ghost." Tales of the Norwegian monkfish, for instance, go back to medieval times. The first one was caught off the coast after a great tempest. It "had a man's face, rude and ungraceful with a bald, shining head; on the shoulders something resembling a monk's cowl; and long winglets instead of arms. The extremity of the body ended in a tail." According to the historian who described it, the monkfish was given to the

Below: a drawing of a kraken in the form a huge sea serpent as reported in 1734 by the Norwegian missionary Hans Egede. His was an eye-witness account, and one of the first by a person whose integrity could hardly be doubted.

King of Poland who took pity on it and had it placed back in the sea.

In 1680 a frightful kraken, which is a legendary giant sea monster, swam too close to the shore of Norway, became jammed in a cleft of rock, and remained there until it died. The stench from the kraken polluted the entire neighborhood, and it was months before the local people could go within miles of the rotting carcass. More than 50 years later, in 1734, another kraken was observed by the celebrated Danish missionary Hans Egede—this time near Greenland. He recorded the experience in his diary stating: "The monster was of so huge a size that, coming out of the water, its head reached as high as a main-mast; its body was as bulky as the ship, and three or four times as long. It had a long pointed snout, and spouted like a whale-fish; it had great broad paws; the body seemed covered with

Below: a suggestion by the 19th-century naturalist Henry Lee of how Egede's kraken could be a partially hidden giant squid.

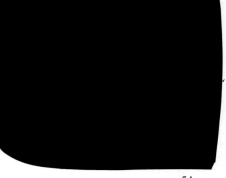

51

Above: a sketch of the head of the sea serpent sighted from the _Daedalus_. This drawing, like

shellwork, and the skin was very ragged and uneven. The under part of its body was shaped like an enormous huge serpent, and when it dived again under the water, it plunged backward into the sea, and so raised its tail aloft, which seemed a whole ship's length distant from the bulkiest part of its body."

Another 18th-century writer on the kraken was the Norwegian Bishop of Bergen, Erik Pontoppidan. He wrote a book about the natrual history of Norway in 1752, and, although he did not see a sea monster himself, he believed the scores of fishermen who told him that they had. He described the kraken as it was described to him. "Its back or upper part, which seems to be about an English mile-and-a-half in circumference, looks at first like a number of small islands surrounded with something that floats and fluctuates like seaweed . . . at last several bright points or horns appear, which grow thicker and thicker the higher they rise above the water. . . . After the monster has been on the surface for a short time it begins slowly to sink again, and then the danger is as great as before, because the motion of his sinking causes such a swell in the sea and such an eddy or whirlpool, that it draws everything down with it . . ."

In 1765, the same year that Bishop Pontoppidan's book appeared in English translation, _The Gentleman's Magazine_ in London stated that "the people of Stockholm report that a great dragon, named Necker, infests the neighboring lake, and seizes and devours such boys as go into the water to wash." This did not stop the Bishop of Avranches from swimming there on a sunny summer day, although the onlookers "were greatly surprised when they saw him return from imminent danger."

With some three-fifths of the earth's surface covered with water, it is hardly surprising that stories of sea monsters arose. Sightings were reported in many parts of the world, including North America after it was settled by Europeans. The coast of New England soon became a popular place for serpent encounters, and between 1815 and 1823, hardly a summer went by without someone meeting up with a sea monster. In June 1815 a strange animal was observed moving rapidly south through Gloucester Bay. Its body, about 100 feet long, seemed to have a string of 30 or 40 humps, each the size of a barrel. It had a head shaped like a horse, and was dark brown in color. Two years later it was again seen in the bay, and the *Gloucester Telegraph* reported: "On the 14th of August the sea serpent was approached by a boat within 30 feet, and on raising its head above water was greeted by a volley from the gun of an experienced sportsman. The creature turned directly toward the boat, as if meditating an attack, but sank down. . . ."

The following year, the same or a similar creature was observed in Nahant. One of the clearest accounts was given by Samuel Cabot of Boston. Mr. Cabot was standing on the crowded Nahant beach when he noticed that a number of boats were speedily making for the shore. "My attention," he wrote, "was suddenly arrested by an object emerging from the water at the distance of about 100 or 150 yards, which gave to my mind at the first glance, the idea of a horse's head. It was elevated

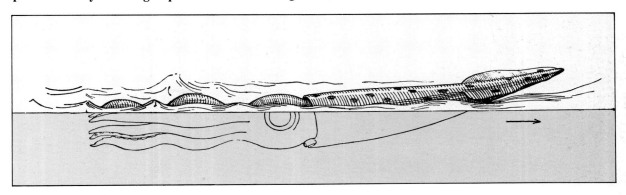

Right: sailors of old went in fear of an attack by a sea monster, as shown in this 18th-century print.

Below: illustration of a sponge diver swallowed whole by a sea monster said to be the size of a small boat. Fear of this monster was reported by the British vice-consul in 1875 as the reason for a sharp drop in the supply of sponges from Mount Lebanon—and a subsequent rise in their price.

Above: in 1891 a sea monster was reported to have appeared suddenly among the bathers at Pablo Beach, Florida, causing great consternation and panic.

Below: the great monster of Lake Utopia surprises two canoeists. Sightings of this huge creature in the Canadian lake have been reported for more than 100 years.

about two feet from the water, and he depressed it gradually to within six or eight inches as he moved along. His bunches appeared to me not altogether uniform in size. I felt persuaded by this examination that he could not be less than 80 feet long." The horse-like monster reappeared again the next summer, and it was watched by dozens of vacationers. "I had with me an excellent telescope," declared one knowledgeable witness, "and . . . saw appear, at a short distance from the shore, an animal whose body formed a series of blackish curves, of which I counted 13 . . . This at least I can affirm . . . that it was neither a whale, nor a cachalot [sperm whale], nor any strong souffleur [dolphin], nor any other enormous cetacean [water mammal]. None of these gigantic animals has such an undulating back."

Within a short while the creature had shown itself to the crew of the sloop *Concord*. The captain and the mate made a deposition of what they had seen before a local Justice of the Peace as soon as they reached shore. In his sworn statement the mate said in part: "His head was about as long as a horse's and was a proper snake's head—there was a degree of flatness, with a slight hollow on the top of his head—his eyes were prominent, and stood out considerably from the surface . . ." The same animal was later seen and identified by Reverend Cheever Finch, who said he spent a half-hour watching its "smooth rapid progress back and forth."

Many lakes are immensely deep, and could provide suitable habitats for large monsters. In fact, the next North American area to be infiltrated by sea serpents was British Columbia, where deep-water lakes are spaced between the Rockies and the Pacific. It was while taking a team of horses across Lake Okanagan in 1854 that an Indian halfbreed claimed to have been "seized by a giant hand which tried to pull me down into the water." He managed to struggle out of the grip, but the horses in his charge were not so lucky. The monster—which apparently had several long and powerful arms—got a hold on the animals and pulled them under the surface; all of them drowned. The sea serpent was known as Naitaka to the Indians and Ogopogo to the settlers. It was seen regularly from then on, and a pioneer named John McDougal later recounted an experience similar to the halfbreed's. Again the man escaped with his life, and again the horses were the victims. By the 1920s the "thing in the lake" was internationally famous, and a London music hall ditty immortalized it with the words: "His mother was an earwig / His father was a whale / A little bit of head / And hardly any tail / And Ogopogo was his name."

From Canada the story of the serpents moved south to the Mormon settlement of Salt Lake City. In July 1860 the newspaper there, *The Desert News*, offered new testimony about the monster of Bear Lake. Up to that time, the Shoshone Indians of Utah had been the principal witnesses of the "beast of the storm spirits," and they were seldom taken seriously. The newspaper story, however, recounted the experience of a respected local resident who had been going along the east shore of the lake. "About half-way," wrote a reporter, "he saw something in the lake which . . . he thought to be a drowned person . . . he rode to the beach and the waves were running pretty high. . . . In a few

The Captain, the Sailing Ship, and the Sea Serpent

From the 1860 report of Captain William Taylor, Master, *British Banner*: "On the 25th of April, in lat. 12 deg. 7 min. 8 sec., and long. 93 deg. 52 min. E., with the sun over the mainyard, felt a strong sensation as if the ship was trembling. Sent the second mate aloft to see what was up. The latter called out to me to go up the fore rigging and look over the bows. I did so, and saw an enormous serpent shaking the bowsprit with his mouth. It must have been at least about 300 feet long; was about the circumference of a very wide crinoline petticoat, with black back, shaggy mane, horn on the forehead, and large glaring eyes placed rather near the nose, and jaws about eight feet long. He did not observe me, and continued shaking the bowsprit and throwing the sea alongside into a foam until the former came clear away of the ship. The serpent was powerful enough, although the ship was carrying all sail, and going at about ten knots at the time he attacked us, to stop her way completely. When the bowsprit, with the jibboom, sails, and rigging, went by the board, the monster swallowed the foretopmast, staysail, jib, and flying-jib, with the greatest apparent ease. He shoved off a little after this, and returned apparently to scratch himself against the side of the ship, making a most extraordinary noise, resembling that on board a steamer when the boilers are blowing off. The serpent darted off like a flash of lightning, striking the vessel with its tail, and staving in all the starboard quarter gallery with its tail. Saw no more of it."

minutes . . . some kind of an animal that he had never seen before . . . raised out of the water. He did not see the body, only the head and what he supposed to be part of the neck. It had ears or bunches on the side of its head nearly as big as a pint cup. The waves at times would dash over its head, when it would throw water from its mouth or nose. It did not drift landward, but appeared stationary, with the exception of turning its head." The next day, July 28, the creature was seen by a man and three women—but this time it was in motion and "swam much faster than a horse could run on land."

Reports of the Bear Lake serpent continued for several decades, but were temporarily eclipsed in 1941 with the advent of Slimey Slim, the serpent that inhabited Lake Payette in Idaho. During July and August that summer more than 30 people—most of them boaters on the lake's seven miles of water—saw the monster. For a while, they kept quiet about it. Then Thomas L. Rogers, City Auditor of Boise, Idaho, decided to speak up. He told a reporter: "The serpent was about 50 feet long and going five miles an hour with a sort of undulating movement. . . . His head, which resembles that of a snub-nosed crocodile, was eight inches above the water. I'd say he was about 35 feet long on consideration."

With the publication of this story the lake was inundated with camera-wielding tourists hoping for a glimpse of Slimey Slim. After an article about him appeared in *Time* magazine, the monster seemed to turn shy, and little more was heard or seen of him. With Slim's disappearance, attention returned to Ogopogo, who, having been seen by a captain in the Canadian Fishery Patrol, had been described as being like "a telegraph pole with a sheep's head." An American visitor to Canada was struck "dumb with horror" on catching sight of the monster. On July 2, 1949, Ogopogo was seen by the Watson family of Montreal together with a Mr. Kray. Newsmen reported of their experience: "What the party saw was a long sinuous body, 30 feet in length, consisting of about five undulations, apparently separated from each other by about a two-foot space . . . . The length of each of the undulations . . . would have been about five feet. There appeared to be a forked tail, of which only one-half came above the water."

Three summers later Ogopogo presented himself to a woman visitor from Vancouver, swimming within a few hundred feet of her. "I am a stranger here," she said shortly afterward. "I did not even know such things existed. But I saw it so plainly. A head like a cow or horse that reared right out of the water. It was a wonderful sight. The coils glistened like two huge wheels. . . . There were ragged edges (along its back) like a saw. It was so beautiful with the sun shining on it. It was all so clear, so extraordinary. It came up three times, then submerged and disappeared."

Reports of the sea serpent mounted until 1964, when Ogopogo apparently went into retirement. However, one of the most graphic accounts of the creature was featured in *The Vernon Advertiser* of July 20, 1959. The writer, R. H. Millar, was the newspaper's owner-publisher, and the sighting of "this fabulous sea serpent" was clearly the highlight of his journalistic life. "Returning from a cruise down Okanagan Lake, traveling at 10 miles an hour, I noticed, about 250 feet in our wake, what appeared to be the serpent," he recorded. "On picking up the field glasses, my thought was verified. It was Ogopogo, and it was traveling a great deal faster than we were. I would judge around 15 to 17 miles an hour. The head was about nine inches above the water. The head is definitely snakelike with a blunt nose. . . . Our excitement was short-lived. We watched for about three minutes, as Ogie did not appear to like the boat coming on him broadside; [he] very gracefully reduced the five humps which were so plainly visible, lowered his head, and gradually submerged. At no time was the tail visible. The family's version of the color is very dark greenish. . . . This sea serpent glides gracefully in a smooth motion . . . . This would lead one to believe that in between the humps it possibly has some type of fin which it works . . . to control direction."

The publicity given to Ogopogo brought eye-witness versions of serpents in other North American lakes, including Flathead Lake in Montana; Lake Walker, Nevada; Lake Folsom, California; and Lake Champlain, Vermont. From Monterey in Southern California came reports of the so-called "monster of San Clemente," who was also known as the Old Man of Monterey. Further north, on Vancouver Island, a serpent nick-

named "Caddy" made a rival bid for the headlines. The most sober and authentic sounding account of Caddy goes back to 1950, when he was seen by Judge James Thomas Brown, then one of Saskatchewan's leading members of the judiciary. He was spending a winter holiday on the island when he, his wife, and daughter spotted Caddy some 150 yards from shore.

"His head [was] like a snake's [and] came out of the water four or five feet straight up," stated the judge. "Six or seven feet from the head, one of his big coils showed clearly. The coil itself was six or seven feet long, fully a foot thick, perfectly round and dark in color. . . . It seemed to look at us for a moment and then dived. It must have been swimming very fast, for when it came up again it was about 300 yards away . . . I got three good looks at him. On one occasion he came up almost right in front of us. There was no question about the serpent—it was quite a sight. I'd think the creature was 35 to 40 feet long. It was like a monstrous snake. It certainly wasn't any of those sea animals we know, like a porpoise, sea-lion and so on. I've seen them and know what they look like."

Monsters of the lakes and seas continued to make appearances in the present century. Passengers and crews of the *Dunbar Castle* in 1930, and again of the *Santa Clara* in 1947, sighted such monsters in the Atlantic. It must have been an added thrill for the passengers as they spotted the serpents swimming nearby. In the summer of 1966, while rowing across the Atlantic in their boat *English Rose III*, Captain John Ridgway and Sergeant Chay Blyth were nearly rammed by one of the marine monsters. It was shortly before midnight on July 25, and Blyth was asleep. Captain Ridgway, who was rowing, was suddenly "shocked to full wakefulness" by a strange swishing noise to starboard.

"I looked out into the water," he recounts in their book *A Fighting Chance*, "and suddenly saw the writhing, twisting shape of a great creature. It was outlined by the phosphorescence in the sea as if a string of neon lights were hanging from

Above: the partially decomposed body of a big sea animal washed ashore on the Massachusetts coast in 1970. It was about 30 feet long and weighed 15–20 tons. Although it had a long neck, it was believed to be a species of whale. Finding dead sea creatures on the shore is fairly common, and big ones keep the monster story alive.

Left: a sea serpent supposedly captured off the coast of England in 1897. Its totally unreal quality and the way the captors are so carefully holding their hands over what could be segment joins make it appear to be a hoax—all in fun from the men's expressions.

Below: a joke photo of Ogopogo, the Canadian lake monster, surfacing for a coffee break in 1960.

it. It was an enormous size, some 35 or more feet long, and it came toward me quite fast. I must have watched it for some 10 seconds. It headed straight at me and disappeared right beneath me. I stopped rowing. I was frozen with terror . . . I forced myself to turn my head to look over the port side. I saw nothing, but after a brief pause I heard a most tremendous splash. I thought this might be the head of the monster crashing into the sea after coming up for a brief look at us. I did not see the surfacing—just heard it. I am not an imaginative man, and I searched for a rational explanation for this incredible occurrence in the night as I picked up the oars and started rowing again . . . I reluctantly had to believe that there was only one thing it could have been—a sea serpent."

As far back as 1820 the English naturalist Sir Joseph Banks, who had sailed around the world with Captain Cook, had given scientific credence and his "full faith" to "the existence of our Serpent of the Sea." He was followed in this a few years later by the botanist and director of Kew Gardens, Sir William J. Hooker, who said of the sea serpent that, "It can now no longer be considered in association with hydras and mermaids, for there has been nothing said with regard to it inconsistent with reason. It may at least be assumed as a sober fact in Natural History . . ."

Below: John Ridgway and Chay Blyth in the *English Rose III*, the small boat in which the two rowed across the Atlantic during the summer of 1966. Ridgway is certain that he saw a 35-foot-long monster which headed straight for the boat one night. It came fast, but disappeared right underneath him as he sat in frozen horror.

Since that time, much has been learned about life underneath the ocean and about the ocean bed itself. In 1865 a Frenchman descended to a depth of 245 feet. Within a hundred years that record was smashed by Dr. Jacques Piccard and Lieutenant D. Walsh of the U.S. Navy. On January 23, 1960, these two men took the bathyscaphe *Trieste* down to a depth of 35,802 feet at Marianas Trench in the Pacific. This is the world's deepest trench and, measured from top to bottom, is higher than Mount Everest. They described the bottom as a "waste of snuff-colored ooze." Being able to go so far into the ocean's depths has increased the chances of an encounter with a deep-sea monster that may date from prehistoric days.

Explorers such as Piccard and the world-famous Captain Jacques Cousteau have seen species of fish that were previously unknown to or unseen by man. Swimming through the deep troughs, trenches, and ridges that make the ocean bed a kind of underwater mountain area, are millions of hitherto unclassified creatures. "I was astounded by what I saw in the shingle at Le Mourillon," writes Cousteau of one of his expeditions, ". . . rocks covered with green, brown, and silver forests of algae, and fishes unknown to me, swimming in crystal clear water. . . . I was in a jungle never seen by those who floated on the opaque roof." In 1969 the world's largest research submarine—the electrically powered *Ben Franklin* designed by Jacques Piccard—drifted to a depth of 600 feet below the Gulf Stream. Its six-man crew surfaced with numerous reports of sightings made through one or another of the craft's 29 viewing ports, including the observation of the tiny purple colored Hatchet fish.

From these and other expeditions it is obvious that man is determined to explore and chart the world beneath the sea. Scientists state that before long some 98 percent of the ocean floor will have been explored, and that such exploration could mean the discovery of any monster or monsters which have been living in the ocean ridges. The U.S. Navy is developing a Deep Submergence Search Vehicle, which will be prepared if it encounters more dangerous inhabitants than the prawns, starfish, and copepods already found to be living in the low-level oozes. Underwater television, sonar sensing equipment, and electronic flash lamps and floodlights will compensate for the lack of light.

Men like Cousteau have pioneered in building underwater houses and villages—such as the U.S. Navy's *Sealab* machines— in which aquanauts can live beneath the oceans for periods of up to 30 days. In Switzerland today there is a special tourist submarine that takes visitors beneath the surface of a lake for a view of the wonders down below. From that it is just another large step to underwater cruise liners which are being planned to take tourists under the waters of the ocean.

In recent years giant sharks whose heads measure some four feet from eye to eye have been photographed on the sea bed. This suggests that even bigger fish—the traditional monsters— are waiting to be found. In their places of so-called eternal darkness, the oceans go down six miles or more—and it is there that the kraken survivors or descendants may lurk. Not long ago a giant pink squid was captured off the coast of Peru. Its 35-

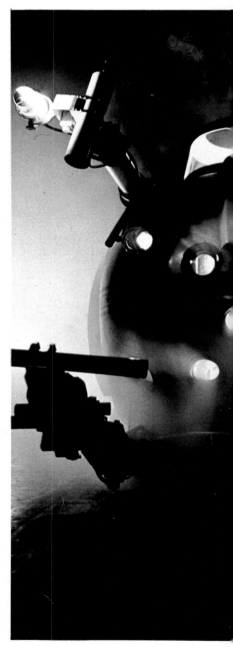

Right: the secrets of the sea may not remain hidden for much longer. As science develops more and more sophisticated equipment to explore the greatest depths, the chances of solving the monster riddle become greater. Here A. B. Rechnitzer (left) and Jacques Piccard are shown on board the *Trieste*, which Piccard piloted to a depth of 18,150 feet. Below: this submersible can carry out maintenance work on undersea wellheads at 2000 feet.

Above: the grotesque hatchet fish, *Argyropelecus hemigymus*, one of the deep-ocean creatures. This monster is less than three inches long, but who knows if it has giant companions in the silent depths?

foot-long tentacles and its eyes of a foot in diameter caused a sensation. Scientists suggest that the pink squid is nothing compared to the creatures that have yet to be caught. To back up their argument, they point to certain pieces of squid that have been taken from the stomach of whales. Projecting the size of the whole squid from the pieces, they say it would be more than 100 feet in length.

It does not seem too fanciful to imagine that one day in the future a nuclear powered submarine, such as the U.S. Navy's *Nautilus*, could be drifting silently beneath the ice cap at the North Pole when it was suddenly attacked by an underwater monster in defense of its home or family. A similar fate could happen to one of the proposed deep-sea cruise liners. No one knows who would emerge the victor, or how many lives might be lost. But one thing is certain. It would make the most sensational sea monster news in centuries—and this time the accounts could not be put down to the imagination or exaggeration of sailors.

4

The Loch Ness Monster

Among lake monsters, Nessie of Loch Ness in Scotland holds a special place. She has been pursued by submarines, featured on front pages, and starred in the movies—but her "stand-in" was the model pictured here.

The African python, which is capable of swallowing a goat, has been seen swimming in the Indian Ocean, sometimes traveling from island to island in search of food. Attempts by large snakes such as this to board passing ships in search of a resting place have naturally given rise to tales of sea monsters. Bits of floating timber or ship-wreck may account for other monster stories. But it is possible that some accounts of sea monsters are genuine. They are disbelieved mainly because the creatures seen have not yet been identified by scientists, or are thought to be long extinct.

About 80 to 90 million years ago giant

63

"A strange creature emerging from the bracken"

reptiles roamed the earth and scoured the oceans in search of food. For survival they depended on brute strength, adaptation to changing environments, and hiding from any danger they could not cope with. For many millions of years the seas were dominated by the fish-eating *plesiosaurus* with its barrel-shaped body and serpentine neck, and the sharklike *ichthyosaur*, or fish lizard. Gradually these animals were displaced by aggressive 40-foot-long sea lizards, the *mosasaurs*. We know that giant land animals began to disappear from the earth, but we do not know what happened to species of animals that were equally at home in the water. Could they have used their skills of adaptation and hiding to penetrate the depths of oceans and lakes and find a way to survive? It is not entirely impossible. After all, huge sea animals really did exist. They are not a figment of our imagination as some skeptics seem to imply. Let us explore the possibilities that may defy the skeptics.

Many of the Scottish lakes, or lochs as they are known in Scotland, are extremely deep. One of the deepest ones, Loch Ness, has become almost legendary because of its associations with repeated sightings of a monster. A dramatic and recent sighting took place in July 1933. Mr. and Mrs. George Spicer were driving home to London along the south bank of Loch Ness when they saw a strange creature emerging from the bracken. It appeared to have a long undulating neck little thicker than an elephant's

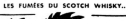

LES FUMÉES DU SCOTCH WHISKY...

...où la véritable origine du monstre de Loch-Ness

Above: a skeptical French cartoon makes the caustic suggestion that Scotch whisky provides the real source for the Loch Ness Monster.

Right: looking across the famous lake from the shoreline. Loch Ness is the largest body of fresh water in Great Britain, and its mean average depth is even twice that of the North Sea. Much of it is 700 feet deep, and it is 734 feet at the deepest recorded spot.

trunk, a tiny head, a thick ponderous body, and four feet or flappers. Carrying what seemed to be a young animal in its mouth, it lurched across the road, lumbered into the undergrowth, and disappeared with a splash into the lake. The whole startling incident lasted only a few seconds, but it left an indelible impression on the couple. Mr. Spicer later described the creature to a newspaper reporter as a "loathsome sight." He said it looked like "a huge snail with a long neck."

Despite the scorn heaped on Mr. Spicer by the leading scientists and zoologists of the day, there were many who believed his story of the 25-to-30-foot-long monster. Indeed, Spicer was not the only nor the first person to have seen—or claimed to have seen—the beast from the deep. Ever since the early 1880s there had been regular sightings of "Nessie," as the Scottish lake monster affectionately became known. Unaccountably, Nessie was popularly regarded as being female. At various times she was seen by a stonemason, a group of schoolchildren, and a forester working for the Duke of Portland. Further appearances were noted in 1912, 1927, and 1930, and descriptions of her personality and activities appeared in newspapers from Glasgow to Atlanta. However, it was not until the summer of 1933—the same summer that the Spicers reported their experience—that Nessie became an international pet. In that year, a new road was built on the north shore of the beast's lake home between Fort William and Inver-

The Creature from the Lake

It was four o'clock in the afternoon on July 22, 1933, and Mr. and Mrs. George Spicer were driving home to London after a tour of the highlands of Scotland. They were halfway between the villages of Dores and Foyer on the south bank of Loch Ness when Mrs. Spicer suddenly noticed something moving out from the bracken on the hillside.

She gave a shriek, and as they watched in horror, a long undulating neck, followed by a ponderous body, lumbered out of the bracken and across the road. It was dark elephant gray. Mr. Spicer said it looked like a huge snail with a long neck. It had a tiny head for its enormous size—about 25 to 30 feet long—and it was carrying what looked like a lamb in its mouth. It seemed to lurch along on flippers as the unbelieving Spicers stared at it. It paid no attention to them, although Mr. Spicer had braked the car hastily and leaped out onto the road. It plunged down a bank toward the lake, and disappeared with a splash into the otherwise still and placid waters. There was no trace left on the road of the incredible creature—just an ordinary man and woman staring at each other stunned, speechless, and very frightened.

ness. According to local inhabitants, Nessie was roused from her sleep hundreds of feet beneath the surface of the lake by the noise of the drilling, the vibrations from the explosions, and the boulders that every now and then crashed down the banks. Annoyed at having her slumber disturbed, she broke water, clambered ashore, and proceeded to roam through the surrounding bracken feasting on any young animals she could get her teeth into.

It was around this period that an Automobile Association patrolman also spotted the sea serpent. He too described it as "a thing with a number of humps above the water line. . . . It had a small head and very long slender neck." Shortly after this a third person—local resident Hugh Gray—actually took a photograph of Nessie, and it was reproduced in newspapers and magazines throughout the world. This photograph, like many that were subsequently taken, was not well-defined. Doubters dismissed the object in the picture as a floating tree trunk or log. For those who accepted this theory, the explanations for the Loch Ness phenomenon was clear: some careless road construction workers had thrown a large piece of wood into the loch. Other disbelievers in the monster's existence preferred to think that someone was trying to pull the public's leg.

In order to seek the truth, journalists from all parts of the globe descended on the area—feature writers and photographers from New York, Rio de Janeiro, and Tokyo among them. They were joined in their watch for the monster by a troop of Boy Scouts. When an old lady disappeared from her home nearby, some said that she had become Nessie's latest victim, and declared that the beast was an agent of the devil. Others asserted that she wouldn't attack a human, and was timid and unaggressive by nature. However, both camps agreed that the monster could change shape at will, that she could rise and sink in the loch vertically, and that her body was iridescent, which made her color vary with the light.

Right: in 1934, the enthusiasm for the Loch Ness monster reached such proportions that the Illustrated London News devoted much of an issue to a discussion of the creature. The cover picture was a drawing made from a sketch by an eyewitness, B. A. Russell. Below: the best-known photograph of Nessie records the long neck and small head reported by many Nessie spotters. It was taken by Kenneth Wilson, a London doctor, on vacation in 1934, and was published in a newspaper. Since then it, and one other successful shot, have been inspected from every angle, analyzed, and argued about.

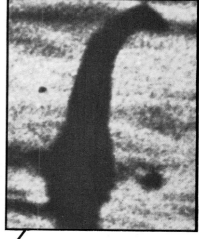

THE ILLUSTRATED LONDON NEWS

The Copyright of all the Editorial Matter, both Engravings and Letterpress, is Strictly Reserved in Great Britain, the Colonies, Europe, and the United States of America.

SATURDAY, JANUARY 13, 1934.

THE "MONSTER" SKETCHED BY MR. B.A. RUSSELL, OF FORT AUGUSTUS.

5ft.

OUR SPECIAL ARTIST INVESTIGATES THE LOCH NESS MONSTER: THE APPEARANCE OF THE MYSTERIOUS CREATURE AS VOUCHED FOR BY MR. B. A. RUSSELL, M.A., OF FORT AUGUSTUS.

In view of the very great interest that is being taken in the so-called Monster of Loch Ness—even in the august pages of our contemporary, "The Times"—we sent our Special Artist, Mr. G. H. Davis, to the Loch, in order that he might record there the evidence of a number of reliable persons who are convinced that they have seen a strange apparition in the waters of the Loch—with the results shown on this page and on two succeeding pages. Our artist's method was to draw the "monster" from a sketch made by the witness concerned; and his drawings were passed as correct by the witnesses. The "monster" depicted above is that vouched for by Mr. B. A. Russell, M.A., of the School House, Fort Augustus. Mr. Russell, a very

calm, level-headed man, states that he saw the mysterious head, as here drawn by himself and by Mr. Davis, on Sunday, October 1, 1933, between 10 and 10.30 in the morning, and that it was visible for twelve minutes. His observation-point was near Captain Meiklem's house, near Fort Augustus, at a height of over 100 feet. The sun, he told our artist, was shining and the Loch was absolutely calm. He watched the head and neck moving with a "horizontal undulation" about five feet above the surface, and noted that the creature covered half a mile during the twelve minutes he had it under view. It was some 700 yards from him and was silhouetted against the pale-grey water, so that it was very evident.

DRAWN BY G. H. DAVIS, OUR SPECIAL ARTIST AT LOCH NESS, FROM A SKETCH BY MR. B. A. RUSSELL, WHO PASSED THE DRAWING AS CORRECT. (SEE ALSO PAGES 40-41 AND 42.)

To support their view that Nessie was alive, well, and dwelling in the lake, her fans produced statistical and historical evidence.

First of all they pointed out that Loch Ness—the largest mass of fresh water in Great Britain—was $22\frac{1}{2}$ miles long and 734 feet deep in the middle. This meant it could easily be the watery home of any huge monster, serpent, or "thing from the deep." They then delved back to the year 565 when a sighting of Niseag—to give Nessie her Gaelic name—was noted by the Irish Saint Columba. For two years previously, Saint Columba had been working to convert the heathen Picts, Scots, and Northumbrians

Below: part of the 1934 issue of the Illustrated London News, presenting a compilation of several eyewitness reports of the popular if elusive monster.

OUR SPECIAL ARTIST INVESTIGATES THE LOCH NESS MONSTER:

DRAWN BY G. H. DAVIS, OUR SPECIAL ARTIST AT LOCH NESS, FROM SKETCHES MADE BY THE WITNESSES.

ACCORDING TO RELIABLE PERSONS WHO ARE CERTAIN THAT THEY HAVE SEEN A MYSTERIOUS

to Christianity from his new monastery on the island of Iona, off the west coast of Scotland. His mission took him throughout the north of the country. When he came to Loch Ness he found some of the local people burying a neighbor who had been badly mauled by the lake monster while out swimming, and who afterward died of his wounds. The corpse had been brought to land by boatmen armed with grappling hooks, but this did not deter one of the missionary's followers from swimming across the narrows at the head of the loch in order to bring over a small boat moored on the other side. Clad only in his loin cloth, the man was making

THE STRANGE CREATURE AS VOUCHED FOR BY EYE-WITNESSES

SEEN BY CAPTAIN R.A.R. MEIKLEM, R.N (RETD) ON AUGUST 5TH 1933, AT ABOUT 5.30 P.M. – END-VIEW OF BACK OF "MONSTER" NEAR CHERRY ISLAND, FORT AUGUSTUS. (FROM A DRAWING MADE UNDER HIS SUPERVISION)

SEEN BY MISS A. SIMPSON, 40 YARDS FROM SHORE, NEAR AULTSAYE, JUNE, 1933. "MONSTER MOVED SLOWLY; TAIL GENTLY MOVING, CAUSING FOAM. (FROM A DRAWING MADE UNDER HER SUPERVISION)

MISS SIMPSON'S SKETCH.

MISS GOODBODY'S SKETCH.

"MONSTER" BEING CAREFULLY OBSERVED BY MR. W.U. GOODBODY & HIS TWO DAUGHTERS FROM 11.45 A.M. TO 12.25 P.M. DECEMBER 30TH, 1933, ABOUT 2½ MILES FROM FORT AUGUSTUS. DISTANCE VARIED BETWEEN 400 & 700 YARDS. (FROM DRAWINGS MADE UNDER THEIR SUPERVISION)

RAPID TURN. OBSERVED MOVEMENTS OF THE "MONSTER"

PLAN OF RAPID TURN.

"MONSTER" MAKING A FINAL RAPID TURN BEFORE BEING HIDDEN FROM VIEW IN SNOWSTORM.

FIRST SEEN BY MISS JANE GOODBODY, 11.30 A.M. DECEMBER 30TH 1933, SHOWING TWO HUMPS.

SEEN BY THE MISSES RATTRAY & MISS HAMILTON NEAR DORES, AUGUST 24TH, 1933, FOLLOWING IN THE WAKE OF THE DRIFTER GRANT HAY. (FROM DETAIL DRAWING)

FLOATING TREE-TRUNK SEEN BY MYSELF & FIVE OBSERVERS AT AULTSAYE ON JANUARY 4TH, 1934, & THOUGHT TO BE THE "MONSTER" UNTIL USING MY BINOCULARS, I DISCOVERED WHAT IT REALLY WAS.

"MONSTER'S" SIZE COMPARED WITH THE DRIFTER. LENGTH 86 FEET. MONSTER 3/4 LENGTH OF DRIFTER.

SECTION OF LOCH NESS (TO SCALE) AT ITS DEEPEST SPOT WIDTH EXACTLY 1 MILE

"SHELVES" IN THE UNDER WATER SIDES OF THE LOCH AS REPORTED BY DIVERS.

THE TEMPERATURE OF THE WATER NEVER FALLS BELOW 39° FAHT.

CREATURE IN LOCH NESS: THE "MONSTER" SKETCHED BY WITNESSES INTERVIEWED

good headway when he was suddenly confronted by a "very odd looking beastie, something like a huge frog, only it was not a frog."

After surfacing and gulping in some air, the monster proceeded to make an open-mouthed attack on the swimmer. She bore down on the defenseless man, and would undoubtedly have swallowed him alive had it not been for the intervention of Columba. Used to dealing with the "irreligious savages," he thought nothing of addressing a monster equally in need of God. With head raised and arms outstretched he commanded: "Go thou no further nor touch the man. Go back at once!" Then, according to an 8th-century biography of the saint, "on hearing this word . . . the monster was terrified and fled away again more

Below: John Cobb, the speedboat racer, shown in the cockpit of his jet-propelled _Crusader_ on Loch Ness in 1952. He was trying to set a world water speed record.

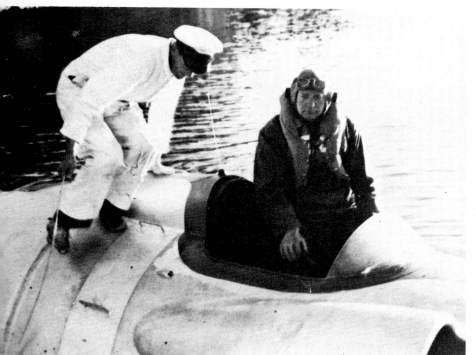

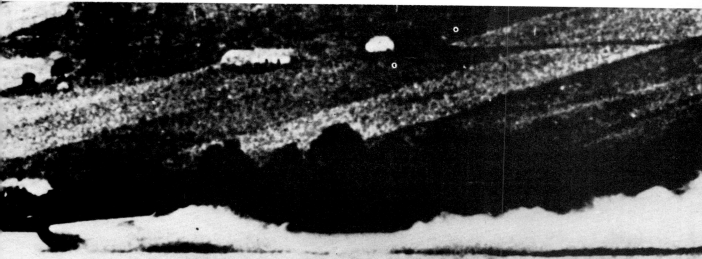

Below: 10 days after failing to break the world record, Cobb set out on Loch Ness to try again. Bottom: seconds after Cobb had succeeded in setting a record on September 29, 1952, he slowed down—and the pressure on his boat at such high speed caused it to break up. Cobb was flung to his death. Eyewitnesses claimed that they saw Nessie's wake at the spot where Cobb slowed, and believed that the creature had ruffled the water when disturbed.

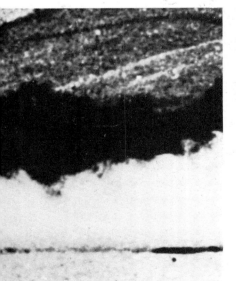

quickly than if it had been dragged on by ropes, though it approached Lugne [the swimmer] as he swam so closely that between man and monster there was no more than the length of one punt pole." This feat was hailed by the potential converts as a manifestation of holy power, and the saint—who was noted everywhere for his "cheerfulness and virtue"—recruited scores of new believers.

From then on the Loch Ness monster became as much a part of Scottish lore as the teachings of Columba himself. At the beginning of the 19th-century, children were warned against playing on the banks of the lake because it was rumored that Nessie was once again restless and about to pounce. Even such a level-headed, no-nonsense person as the novelist Sir Walter Scott perpetuated monster stories. On November 23, 1827, he wrote in his journal: "Clanronald told us . . . that a set of his kinsmen—believing that the fabulous 'water-cow' inhabited a small lake near his house—resolved to drag the monster into day. With this in view, they bivouacked by the side of the lake in which they placed, by way of nightbait, two small anchors such as belong to boats, each baited with the carcass of a dog, slain for the purpose. They expected the water-cow would gorge on the bait and were prepared to drag her ashore the next morning when, to their confusion, the baits were found untouched."

Perhaps the lake monster cleverly avoided the trap. In any case she seems to show herself only when she wants to, often unexpectedly. A few decades later, in 1880, a diver named Duncan McDonald came across the beast while attempting to salvage a boat wrecked on Loch Ness. "I was underwater about my work," he said, "when all of a sudden the monster swam by me as cool and calm as you please. She paid no heed to me, but I got a glance at one of her eyes as she went by. It was small, gray and baleful. I would not have liked to have displeased or angered her in any way!" By then the major feeling about Nessie was that although ugly of face and bad-tempered when aroused, she did not go out of her way to trouble or frighten people.

Another 19th-century account of the Loch Ness monster gives an entirely different view of the lake inhabitant. It said: "A noted demon once inhabited Loch Ness and was a source of terror to the neighborhood. Like other kelpies [water-spirits in the shape of a horse] he was in the habit of browsing along the roadside, all bridled and saddled, as if waiting for someone to mount him. When any unwary traveler did so, the kelpie took to his heels, and presently plunged into deep water with his victim on his back." The teller of this tale mustered up few believers, perhaps because of the great disparity between his description and the more generally accepted ones.

Coming up to the 1930s period when Nessie was at the peak of her popularity, hotelier John Mackay sighted the lake serpent on May 22, 1933. He said that he saw the lake animal make the water "froth and foam" as she reared her ludicrously small head in the air. Although Mackay beat the Spicers by two months in his encounter with Nessie, it was George Spicer's story that was most listened to and believed in nonprofessional quarters.

Before the year 1933 was out Loch Ness and its celebrated inhabitant had become one of the principal tourist attractions of

Great Britain. Holiday makers by the thousands got into their cars and headed north to park along the shores of the lake and gaze out over the water. Between 1933 and 1974, some 3000 people attested to having spotted Nessie as she surfaced, dived, or swam tranquilly along. Claims were also made that the monster made a sound—a cry of "anger and anguish" when nearly run down by a car. Waiting for Nessie rivaled watching flagpole squatters and marathon dancers, which were big vogues of the mid-30s. Hundreds of sun-dazzled or fog-smeared photographs—with an indistinct blur in them—were offered as Nessie at play. The eager Nessie-hunters were given short shrift by E. G. Boulenger, Director of the Aquarium in the London Zoo. He wrote in October 1933 that:

"The case of the Loch Ness monster is worthy of our consideration if only because it presents a striking example of mass hallucination . . . For countless centuries a wealth of weird and eerie legend has centered around this great inland waterway . . . Any person with the slightest knowledge of human nature should therefore find no difficulty in understanding how an animal, once said to have been seen by a few persons, should shortly after have revealed itself to many more."

Another reason for so many sightings was suggested by the more cynical, who pointed to the rewards being offered for the capture of Nessie alive. The money prizes included one for $500 from the New York Zoo, £20,000 ($50,000 at today's exchange rate) from the Bertram Mills circus, and a mammoth £1 million ($2½ million) from the makers of Black and White Whisky. The whisky firm stipulated that the monster, if taken, had to be declared genuine by officials of the British Museum. Debate on Nessie even reached the British House of Commons, and, on November 12, 1933, a member of Parliament called for an official investigation to settle the "monster matter" for once and all. The Government spokesman who replied stated that such an

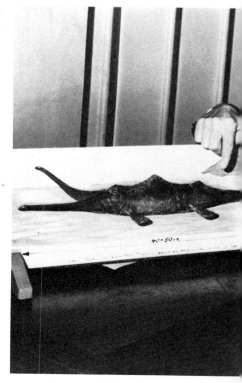

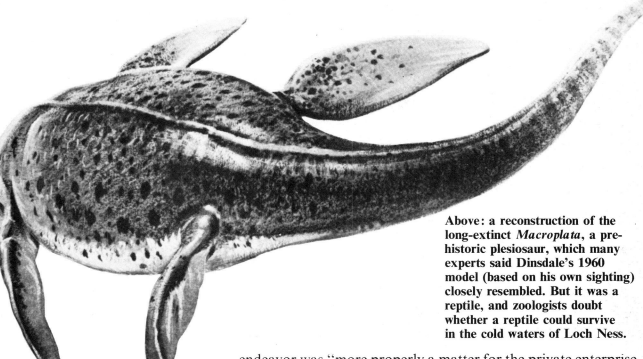

Above: a reconstruction of the long-extinct *Macroplata*, a prehistoric plesiosaur, which many experts said Dinsdale's 1960 model (based on his own sighting) closely resembled. But it was a reptile, and zoologists doubt whether a reptile could survive in the cold waters of Loch Ness.

endeavor was "more properly a matter for the private enterprise of scientists aided by the zeal of the press and photographers."

It was on the same day of the government debate that Mr. Hugh Gray took the famous picture mentioned before. It was published first of all in the Scottish *Daily Record*, and then reproduced throughout the world. That was all the confirmation Nessie's admirers needed. According to Gray, he was walking along the loch shore near Foyers, camera in hand, when, from his vantage point on a 30-foot-high cliff, he saw the quiet water beneath him "explode into commotion." A huge form reared in front of him and a long neck stretched out. During the few seconds that the monster was on the surface, Mr. Gray took five hasty shots of her. Due to the spray that was thrown up, the "object of considerable dimensions" was not clearly discerned. Later, four of the five negatives proved to be blank. The good negative was shown to technical experts of the Kodak camera company, who testified that it had not been tampered with in any way—and once again only the professional zoologists remained dissatisfied. Mr. J. R. Norman of the British Museum stated that "the possibilities leveled down to the object being a bottlenose whale, one of the larger species of shark, or just mere wreckage." Professor Graham Kerr of Glasgow University considered the photograph to be "unconvincing as a representation of a living creature."

A local bailiff, Alexander Campbell, held stage center in June 1934 when he told his Nessie tale. According to him, he had been out fishing in a row boat with two friends when a "dark gray, rocklike hump" rose from the water, stayed there for a moment, and then submerged without causing more than a few ripples. (Campbell was persistent if not consistent. In 1958 he said that Nessie had again appeared before him, but this time she created a "small tidal wave" that sent him toppling into the lake.)

In 1934, too, came the first of the numerous books about the celebrated Loch Ness monster. It listed 47 sightings complete

Above: the endless watch on Loch Ness. Experts estimate that there is one sighting for every 350 hours spent watching the lake.

Below: even at night Nessie is pursued. An expedition in 1970 used this infra-red camera for seeing 100 yards in total dark.

with drawings and photographs. In January a newsreel film said to be of Nessie was shown in London to a private audience. The camera caught her about 100 yards away as she swam past. Of this event *The Times* on January 4 said: "The most clearly evident movements are those of the tail or flukes. This appendage is naturally darker than the body. The photographers describe the general color of the creature as gray, that of the tail as black. Indeterminate movements of the water beside the monster as it swims suggests the action of something in the nature of fins or paddles." Unfortunately, this film disappeared before any study of its authenticity was made.

Three months later Nessie reached the attention of royalty when the Duke of York—who became King George VI—addressed the London Inverness Association, and told members:

"Its [Nessie's] fame has reached every part of the earth. It has entered the nurseries of this country. The other day, I was in the nursery, and my younger daughter, Margaret Rose [now Princess Margaret], aged three, was looking at a fairy-story picture book. She came across a picture of a dragon, and described it to her mother: 'Oh, look Mummy, what a darling little Loch Ness monster!'"

The Abbot of the Monastery in Fort Augustus, at the foot of the loch, added his opinion to the controversy with his announcement that, "the monster is a true amphibian, capable of living either on land or in water, with four rudimentary legs or paddles, an extraordinarily flexible neck, broad shoulders and a strong, broad, flat tail, capable of violently churning the waters around it." Then, in April 1934, came the famous "surgeon's picture" taken by a London surgeon named Kenneth Wilson. He had a telephoto lens on his camera for his hobby of photographing trains. While driving south from a vacation in northern Scotland, he stopped the car at 7:30 a.m. and got out to stretch his legs. He was on a slope 200 feet above the surface of Loch Ness when he suddenly saw the water begin to swirl, and spotted "the head of some strange animal rising." He ran back to the car, returned with the three-quarter plate camera, and rapidly took four pictures. Two of them turned out to be duds, but one showed the monster's long, arched neck, and the last plate revealed its out-of-proportion small head about to submerge. The picture of the head and neck appeared in the London *Daily Mail*. As so often in the past, the public showed interest, but the authorities remained skeptical.

How can a creature of Nessie's size hide out so well in a lake, even one as large as Loch Ness? Part of the answer is that this lake is the receptacle of peat particles from 45 mountain streams and five rivers. Little is visible below a depth of six feet, and underwater exploration by lung divers is stymied by the dense, impenetrable murk. For the most part, Nessie has been seen as a series of humps when she came up from the depths for air. This proved the case with the investigation backed by the insurance tycoon Sir Edward Mountain, who kept an intense five-week watch on the loch in the summer of 1934. Of the 17 monster sightings reported, 11 of them were of humps. This was also true when a Glendoe sawmill worker saw Nessie at 9 a.m. that same summer. He reported a series of 12 humps "each a foot out of water." He said in an article in the *Scotsman* of July 6, 1934: "The day was so clear that I could distinguish drops of water as they fell when the monster shook itself. It reached Glendoe Pier and stretched its neck out of the water where a stream enters the loch. It did not actually come ashore, but seemed to be hunting about the edge, and I cannot see how it could move as it did without using flippers or feet."

The start of World War II in 1939 put an end to speculation about lake serpents for a time, and it wasn't until the early 1950s that Nessie made news again. Then came the usual spate of sightings and photographs. An account of one of the sightings appeared in *Harper's Magazine* in 1957. The witness, Mr. David Slorach, told how he had been driving to Inverness for a business appointment on the morning of February 4, 1954. On looking to his right to admire the view of Loch Ness, he saw something unusual in the water. Its shape reminded him of a "comic ornament popular at one time—a china cat with a long neck. The thing ahead of me looked exactly like the neck and head part. One black floppy 'ear' fell over where the eye might be, and four black streaks ran down the 'neck' . . . The object [was] traveling through the water at great speed, throwing up a huge wave behind. I slowed to around 35 miles per hour, but the object raced ahead and was soon out of sight behind a clump of trees."

Inspired by the renewed interest in Nessie, the BBC sent a television team equipped with a sonic depth-finder to the loch in an attempt to prove or disprove the legend. Obligingly, a "mysterious object" came into range, was recorded some 12 feet below the surface, and was followed to a depth of 60 feet before it lost the depth finder. Experts of the British Museum and the Zoological Society of London were asked their opinions, but they scoffed at the idea of an unfamiliar beast. Instead they spoke of sturgeons, fin whales, sperm whales, and that old standby, the tree trunk. One man was not convinced by the scoffing professionals, however. This was the author and journalist F. W. Holiday. As he put it, his "consuming interest in the problem of the Loch Ness Orm or monster began in 1933 when I was 12 years old." One morning 29 years later, in August 1962, he settled himself on a hillside near Foyers, and, with his binoculars, waited for the monster to make an appearance. He described what happened in his book *The Great Orm of Loch Ness*:

"A dozen or so yards into the loch, opposite the leat [a water channel] an object made a sudden appearance. It was black and glistening and rounded, and it projected about three feet above the surface. Instantly it plunged under again, violently, and produced an enormous upsurge of water. A huge circular wave raced toward me as if from a diving hippopotamus . . . Just below the surface, I then made out a shape. It was thick in the middle and tapered toward the extremities. It was a sort of blackish-gray in color . . . When a chance puff of wind touched the surface, it disappeared in a maze of ripples; but when the water stilled, it was always there. Its size—judging from the width of the leat— was between 40 and 45 feet long."

Holiday also recorded that a film taken at the loch in 1960 was later shown to specialists at the Ministry of Defense's Joint Air Reconnaissance Intelligence Center. After carefully studying and analyzing the images—which showed the customary humped

Above: a Japanese skin diver is poised in readiness to snap a picture of Nessie in her home. A Japanese team went to Loch Ness to hunt the monster in 1973.

Below: in spite of the murkiness of the peat-laden waters of the loch, there have been underwater sightings. Here a strobe camera caught a flipper of a 30-foot-long creature in August 1972.

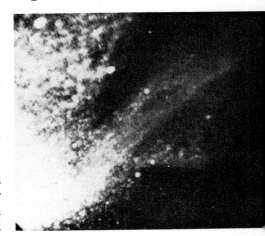

Above: an American skipper, Dan Taylor, and a British crew on his home-made mini-submarine in which they plumbed the depths of Loch Ness to find Nessie in 1969. Taylor's expedition was sponsored by an American encyclopedia firm.

object moving through the water—the experts decided that something, if not Nessie, existed in the deep. They came to the conclusion that the subject of the film "probably is an animate object." However, Nessie came the nearest to getting a certificate of authenticity in 1963 when on the evening of February 2 Grampian and Border Television, an independent British station, transmitted a program about her. The program was presented as a panel discussion, and one of the participants was David James, a Highland laird and a Member of Parliament at the time. He had a few months before kept a two-week, round-the-clock watch on the shores of the loch. Mr. James, founder of "The Loch Ness Phenomena Investigation Bureau," told viewers that his watch had been successful. He said:

"On October 19 [1962], in the middle of the afternoon, we had seven people at Temple Pier, and suddenly everyone was alerted by widespread activity among the salmon. After a few minutes the salmon started panicking—porpoising out in the middle of the loch—and immediately we were aware that there was an object following the salmon which was seen by practically everyone there for three or four minutes." On hearing that—and after sifting through years of recorded evidence—the panel announced that: "We find that there is some unidentified animate object in Loch Ness which, if it be mammal, reptile, fish, or mollusc of any known order, is of such a size as to be worthy of careful scientific examination and identification. If it is not of a known order, it represents a challenge which is only capable of being answered by controlled investigation on carefully scientific principles."

Six years after this television program, in August 1968, a team from the Department of Electronic Engineering of Birmingham University mounted a sonar system on one of the piers on the loch. The scan was directed at the southeast corner, and, according to author Holiday, the scientists achieved "dramatic success." The cathode display screen was photographed every 10 seconds by a movie camera, but for some days, nothing of interest was seen. Then, at 4:30 on the afternoon of August 28, there occurred a remarkable 13-minute sequence. "A large object rose rapidly from the floor of the loch at a range of .8 kilometer, its speed of ascent being about 100 feet a minute," Holiday wrote. "It was rising obliquely away from the sonar source at a velocity of about 6.5 knots, and was soon 1 kilometer away. Its upward movement had now slowed to about 60 feet a minute. This object then changed direction to move toward the pier at about 9 knots, keeping constant depth. Finally, it plunged to the bottom at about 100 feet a minute before rising again at .6 kilometer range, when it apparently moved out of the sonar beam and was lost to record. Meanwhile, a second large object had been detected at .5 kilometer from the pier which finally dived at the astonishing velocity of 450 feet a minute. Both objects remained many feet below the surface."

One of the leaders of the team, Dr. H. Braithwaite, later wrote a magazine article on the sonar experiment in which he stated that, "the high rate of ascent and descent makes it seem very unlikely [that the objects were shoals of fish], and fishery biologists we have consulted cannot suggest what fish they might

Left: the mini-submarine *Pisces* in 1969 in another underwater search for Nessie and the final answer to it all. *Pisces*, which was sponsored by an English newspaper, could stay under the surface for more than 12 hours, and was equipped with a sonar system. Skin divers were among the crew. Below: Elliott Sinclair, one of the *Pisces* team, inside the sub. He is surrounded by the electronic equipment designed to detect any sign of Nessie—who didn't show.

be. It is a temptation to suppose they must be the fabulous Loch Ness monsters, now observed for the first time in their underwater activities."

There the matter rested and there—admired or maligned, sought-after or ignored—lies Nessie. Among the latest to try to explain her away is Dr. Roy Mackal of the Biochemistry Department of the University of Chicago. On visiting Loch Ness in 1966, he suggested that the monster was most likely some kind of "giant sea slug." Four years later another American, Dr. Robert Rines of the Massachusetts Academy of Applied Science, took a Klein side-scan sonar to the banks of the loch. In the deeper water he detected several large moving objects, and said afterward in a radio interview: "We wouldn't have been here if we didn't have the suspicion that there is something very large in this loch. My own view now, after having personal interviews with, I think, highly reliable people, is that there is an amazing scientific discovery awaiting the world here in Loch Ness."

However, Loch Ness is far from being the only fresh-water lake with a quota of monsters. Loch Morar, some 30 miles to the west and completely separated from Loch Ness, has its own Great Worm. At the beginning of 1970 a scientific team headed by the British biologist Dr. Neill Bass began a survey of the site. The team's efforts were rewarded on the afternoon of July 14 when Dr. Bass and two colleagues went for a walk on the north shore of the loch. It started to rain and, while his companions sheltered under some nearby trees, Bass gazed out over the rain-flecked water. Then, just as the weather improved and a breeze came up, the surface was broken by a "black, smooth-looking hump-shaped object." It was some 300 yards away, and by the time his fellow scientists had joined him, the creature had submerged vertically. Thirty seconds later, however, there was another disturbance in the water. It was followed by what the survey's final report called "a spreading circular wake or ripple which radiated across the waves to about 50 yards diameter." For a while Bass thought the object might have been a giant eel, but then realized that the movement was uncharacteristic of such a fish. In the end the report declared it to be "an animate object of a species with which he [Bass] was not familiar in this type of habitat."

The following month a zoology student, Alan Butterworth, also spotted the monster through binoculars while keeping watch on Loch Morar. The water was calm, and visibility was good. The watcher observed a "dark-colored hump," dome-shaped and similar to a rocky islet. The object was about $1\frac{1}{2}$ miles away. Butterworth left to get his camera, and when he returned with it the Great Worm had disappeared. So the most important goal— to obtain authentic film of the monster—was not fulfilled.

Not to be outdone by Scotland, countries from France to Australia to Argentina have claimed that their inland lakes contain their own mysterious and outsized monsters. Ireland, whose legends of lake monsters go back to ancient times, easily heads the list.

Another region with a long tradition of lake monster stories is Scandinavia. It was while visiting Scandinavia and Iceland in 1860 that the English clergyman and author Reverend Sabine Baring-Gould heard of the Skrimsl, a "half-fabulous" monster said to inhabit some of the Icelandic lakes. Although he didn't see any of the beasts himself, he spoke to educated and respectable lawyers and farmers who told of one particular Skrimsl. It was almost 50 feet long and apparently looked much like the more famous Nessie. "I should have been inclined to set the whole story down as a myth," wrote Baring-Gould, "were it not for the fact that the accounts of all the witnesses tallied with remarkable minuteness, and the monster is said to have been seen not in one portion of the lake (the Lagarflot) only, but at different points."

The clergyman also learned of a similar creature in Norway—a

Right: Frank Searle, one of Nessie's most determined hunters. He first saw the monster in 1965, gave up his job four years later, and moved to Loch Ness to camp by the lakeside in hopes of getting absolute proof of her existence. He claimed 18 sightings by 1972. Searle spent up to 19 hours a day waiting by the side of the loch, camera poised and at the ready.
Left: one of the photographs taken of Nessie at home in 1972 by the persistent Frank Searle.

Left: another Searle photograph of the dim humps of the monster.

Below: even in the depths of winter, Searle keeps vigil. This photo was taken January 8, 1974.

51213

Top: one of the special effects crew working on the enormous mechanical Loch Ness Monster created for a 1969 movie, _The Private Life of Sherlock Holmes_, filmed in Scotland. During the shooting the mechanical Nessie disappeared into the depths of the lake, presumably to provide a bizarre companion for the real Nessie lurking somewhere in the dark, mysterious loch herself. Above: a still from the film as the mechanical monster encounters Dr. Watson, Holmes, and Gabrielle in a small boat.

slimy, gray-brown animal that terrified the people living around Lake Suldal. Its head was said to be as big as a row boat. The story was told of a man who, crossing the lake in a small craft, was set upon by the monster and seized by the arm. The attacker let go only when the victim recited the Lord's Prayer. But the man's arm was mangled and useless thereafter.

In Sweden itself Lake Storsjö has long been associated with monsters, and a turn-of-the-century zoologist, Dr. Peter Olsson, spent several years analyzing and sifting through 22 reports containing numerous sightings. The Lake Storsjö monster, or leviathan, was said to be white-maned and reddish in color, more like an enormous seahorse than anything else. It was first spotted in 1839 by some farmers, and reports of it continued well into the 20th-century. The creature differed from its fellows by virtue of its speed, which was estimated at a rapid 45 m.p.h. Olsson regarded it as "the fastest and most fascinating of all lake dwellers," a view which was shared by the _New York Times_ in 1946. Under the heading, "Normalcy?," an article in the paper stated that, after the insanity of World War II, things were getting back into their old familiar and comforting routine because monsters were being seen again.

Shortly afterward a Stockholm newspaper reported that a group of three people had seen the Lake Storsjö monster when the lake's "calm shining surface was broken by a giant snakelike object with three prickly dark humps. It swam at a good parallel to the shore, on which the waves caused by the object were breaking." More sightings were reported in 1965. This inspired the local tourist board to use a color picture of the monster in its brochures, and to boast that the beast was Sweden's answer to the Loch Ness monster.

Ireland is Scotland's nearest rival in the "creature in the lake" stakes, however. There are innumerable reports, accounts, and twice-told tales about such beings. In recent times the stories have proved as vivid and interesting as ever. For example, there is the one of three Dublin priests. On the evening of May 18, 1960, Fathers Daniel Murray, Matthew Burke, and Richard Quigly went trout fishing off Lake Ree—called Lough Ree in Ireland—on the River Shannon. They were exceedingly pleased with the warmth, the calmness of the water, and the way the fish were biting. All at once the tranquility was shattered by the approach of a large flat-headed animal they couldn't identify. It was about 100 yards from where they sat. When it swam up the lake toward them, the startled priests jumped to their feet. "Do you see what I see," one of them cried out, and the other two nodded their heads in amazement. "It went down under the water," stated one of the priests later, "and came up again in the form of a loop. The length from the end of the coil to the head was six feet. There was about 18 inches of head and neck over the water. The head and neck were narrow in comparison to the thickness of a good-sized salmon. It was getting its propulsion from underneath the water, and we did not see all of it."

Lough Ree, where this sighting took place, is one of many small lakes in Ireland, whose west coast is dotted with them. Each lake it seems has its own particular inhabitant. It was this fact which in the 1960s inspired Captain Lionel Leslie, an explorer and cousin of Sir Winston Churchill, to mount his own investigation of the monsters. In October 1965 he went to Lough Fadda in Galway, and exploded a small charge of gelignite against a rock. He hoped that this would bring a *Peiste*, or lake monster, to the surface. Sure enough, a few seconds later a large black object appeared some 50 yards from the shore. Dismissing the possibility of it being a piece of wood or debris, Captain Leslie later told a reporter from *The Irish Independent*, "I am satisfied beyond any doubt that there is a monster in Lough Fadda." A subsequent netting operation failed to capture the creature. Captain Leslie tried again in 1969. In the company of author F. W. Holiday, he plumbed the depths of Loughs Shanakeever, Auna, and Nahooin, but came up with nothing. Television cameras were on hand to record the hoped-for event, but all they were able to film was Captain Leslie, his disheartened band of monster hunters, and the constant rain.

Such experiences—even though they make ready fodder for newspapers and TV—tend to lessen scientific belief in the existence of lake creatures. John Wilson, warden of the bird sanctuary operated by the Royal Society for the Protection of Birds in Lancashire, England, is another skeptic. Writing in the Society's journal in the summer of 1974, he says that Nessie, and presumably those like her, could well be a group of otters at play. "Four or five otters swimming in line with heads, bodies, and tails continually appearing and disappearing combine to look like a prehistoric monster," he states.

For the steady line of Nessie-spotters since George Spicer hit the headlines in 1933, the Loch Ness monster is very much a reality. For the disbelievers, explanations like Dr. Mackal's sea slug or Mr. Wilson's otters are perfectly logical and satisfactory. What is the real truth? No one knows yet!

Below: a photograph of Nessie that is clearer than most. It was taken by a resident of Inverness, Scotland, on a sightseeing trip to Loch Ness with visitors in 1969.

Did the Dinosaurs Survive?

Because most of the world has been mapped out, we tend to forget that much still remains to be explored. Geographers may take bearings from distant mountain ranges, follow a river along its banks, or photograph regions from the air. However, they will not usually penetrate huge areas of swamp or forest, climb inaccessible peaks, or plumb the depths of lakes. Even discounting the vast wastes of Antarctica, nearly a tenth of the earth's land surface remains almost totally unexplored. Who can guess what lies in the unknown?

In the last 150 years, many new large animals have been discovered. Some, like

Every schoolchild knows that huge and fierce dinosaurs once roamed the face of the earth. The question now is whether there are still some stray survivors of that monstrous species living in the caves and jungles of little-known and unexplored areas—ready to attack. Right: an Asian dinosaur of giant size and frightening strength. It had powerful jaws and big pointed teeth that could tear its victims to pieces. This monster, which reached the overwhelming size of 20 feet high and 45 feet long, moved firmly on strong hindlegs.

Z. Burian 70

"Harrowing adventure in the heart of West Africa"

Below: Ivan T. Sanderson, the naturalist and writer who spent most of his life in exotic and inaccessible parts of the world, photographed with one of his less frightening animal friends during a program for children.

the king cheetah, have been found in areas close to habitation and well-traveled by zoologists and big-game hunters. They had, for some reason, escaped notice. Others, such as the okapi, had taken refuge in remote and difficult country. Because they were believed to be extinct, descriptions of them by local residents had at first been discounted. It is always exciting to find a new species; but to discover that an animal, thought to have been long vanished, still survives is even more thrilling. It is as if, in a reassuring way, it had somehow managed to overcome both the forces of nature and our technological world.

If there is any likelihood of finding other living animals that we thought would never be seen again, it is in unexplored and difficult territory where they may have fled from the competition of newer and more successful species. We know that huge dinosaurs and giant reptiles became extinct about 60 million years ago, probably due to climatic changes that affected their food supply. But what happened to their smaller relatives needing less food? Were they able to find a better area and slowly adapt to changes? Perhaps so. For, although most of the world has undergone violent geological changes in the last 60 million years, Central Africa—hot and swampy—has remained geologically stable. It is essentially the same land mass it was when the giants roamed the earth, much of it almost impenetrable and unexplored. If any creature has survived from the age of dinosaurs it is here that it would be found. It is certainly here that tales of dinosaurs and other massive monsters abound and persist. Those who tell the tales are often respected scientists.

The well-known naturalist and writer Ivan T. Sanderson, for example, recounts a harrowing adventure on the Mainyu River in the heart of West Africa. The river ran "straight as a man-made canal," and Sanderson's canoe glided along with the paddles hardly being used. Ahead of him, in the lead canoe, was his fellow explorer and animal collector Gerald Russell. A hundred feet of water separated the two boats as they approached a deep shadowy gorge hemmed in by sheer high walls and huge black caves. The two explorers had only recently ventured that far inland, and their two African aides—Ben and Bassi—were equally strange to the area. The adventurers were near the middle of the winding mile-and-a-half-long gorge when their smooth progress was abruptly disturbed. "The most terrible noise I have heard short of an oncoming earthquake or the explosion of an aerial torpedo at close range, suddenly burst from one of the big caves on my right," declared Sanderson in his book *More "Things."* "Ben, who was sitting up front in our little canoe . . . immediately dropped backward into the canoe. Bassi in the lead canoe did likewise, but Gerald tried to about-face in the strong swirling current, putting himself broadside to the current. I started to paddle like mad, but was swept close to the entrance of the cave from which the noise had come."

A few moments later, when both canoes were opposite the mouth of the cave, an ear-splitting roar came out of it. In Sanderson's own words: "Something enormous rose out of the water, turning it to sherry-colored foam, and then, again roaring, plunged below. This 'thing' was shiny black and was the *head* of something, shaped like a seal but flattened from above to below. It was about the size of a full-grown hippopotamus—this head, I mean. We exited from the gorge at a speed that would have done credit to the Harvard Eight, and it was not until we entered the pool (from which the Mainyu stretched north) that Bassi and Ben came to."

Sanderson and Russell asked the two Africans about the monster, but, not being river people, they could provide no answer. Finally, however, they both yelled "M'koo-m'bemboo," grabbed their paddles, and sped across the pool. The group soon rejoined the rest of its 20-strong party. The other Africans were all local men, and showed great concern over their leaders' frightening experience. The river people among them confirmed Bassi and Ben's opinion that the dreadful creature was one of the M'koo. Said Sanderson: "These animals lived there all the time, they told us, and that is why there were no crocodiles or hippos in the Mainyu. (There were hundreds of both in the pool, the other river, and the Cross River.) But, they went on, M'koo does not eat flesh, but only the big liana fruits and the juicy herbage by the river."

Ivan Sanderson's fantastic encounter with a monster occurred in 1932, and he never did find out the exact nature of the gigantic thing that had so dramatically displayed itself. It is difficult to dismiss his experience as the product of an overstimulated imagination, for Sanderson's story has been accepted by a number of experts in the monster field. Among them is the reputable zoologist and author Dr. Bernard Heuvelmans, who refers to the incident in his wide-ranging and definitive book *On the Track of Unknown Animals*. In this book Heuvelmans stresses that the sighting of the M'koo and other monster evidence came from "a first-rate naturalist whose works are authorities all over the world." Indeed, as a well-traveled and well-informed expert in such matters, Sanderson knew that there had been a "very curious going-on in Africa for more than a century." What he had seen and heard led him to ask: could there still be dinosaurs living in some remoter corners of the African continent, and in other isolated parts of the earth?

To Sanderson, this idea was not too startling—even though dinosaurs are one of a group of huge reptiles that lived during Mesozoic times some 70 to 220 million years ago. After all, he and others had seen what could have been a monster left over from prehistoric times, and he felt that Africa was still a relatively unexplored continent. "Its vast jungle and swamplands have been by-passed in all the modern hubbub," he stated in *More "Things"* in 1969, "and thousands of locations that were fairly well known 50 years ago have now been virtually lost. The mere size of the place is quite beyond comprehension to those who have not visited it, so it is quite useless to suggest that there is not room in it for all manner of things as yet unknown." For proof of this, Sanderson and his fellow explorers did not need to go back further than 1913 when the German government sent a special expedition to its colony in the mountainous Cameroons. The expedition was led by Captain Freiherr von Stein, and its purpose was to make a general survey, map the area, and pinpoint the whereabouts of its vegetable and mineral fields.

Because of the outbreak of World War I the report was never

Was It Really a Dinosaur?

As recently as 1932 a Swedish rubber plantation overseer came across a huge monster in Central Africa. Out hunting in the swampy Kasai valley, J. C. Johanson and his African bearer suddenly saw a creature about 16 yards long with a lizard's head and tail. The men started for home without waiting to see more, but in crossing a swamp on the way they again stumbled on the giant. It was tearing lumps of flesh from a rhinoceros it had killed.

"It was simply terrifying," Johanson later wrote ". . . At first I was careful not to stir, then I thought of my camera. I could plainly hear the crunching of rhino bones in the lizard's mouth. Just as I clicked, it jumped into deep water. The experience was too much for my nervous system. Completely exhausted, I sank down behind the bush that had given me shelter. Blackness reigned before my eyes. . . . I must have looked like one demented when at last I regained camp . . . waving the camera about in a silly way and emitting unintelligible sounds . . . For eight days I lay in a fever, unconscious nearly all the time."

The photographs Johanson had snapped came out, but were not very clear. Might they really have been of a dinosaur that had survived extinction?

published, but the contents of the manuscript were later made available to those in search of sensational monster material. Captain von Stein, a disciplined and hard-headed soldier, wrote in the report that the people who lived by the rivers told him of a "very mysterious thing" that dwelt in the water. In his book *Exotic Zoology*, scientist Willy Ley quotes from the von Stein report. He points out that the captain recorded the experiences of respected guides who, without knowing each other, gave the same details and "characteristic features" about the water beast.

The creature—which at the time of the expedition was spotted in a section of the Sanga River previously said to be non-navigable—was described as of a "brownish-gray color with a smooth skin, its size approximately that of an elephant . . . It is said to have a long and very flexible neck and only one tooth, but a very long one; some say it is a horn. A few spoke about a long muscular tail like that of an alligator. Canoes coming near it are said to be doomed; the animal is said to attack the vessels at once and to kill the crews, but without eating the bodies. The creature is said to live in the caves that have been washed out by the river . . . It is said to climb the shore even at daytime in search of food; its diet is said to be entirely vegetable."

The fact that the monster was a vegetarian convinced von Stein that it was more likely to be a factual beast than a mythical one. The outsized animals of mythology showed no such reluctance to tear human flesh, drink blood, and crunch bones. His belief was strengthened when he was shown the creature's favorite food, "a kind of liana with large white blossoms, with a milky sap and apple-like fruits." He was also taken to a spot by another river where the monster had apparently trampled a fresh path in order to reach the food it liked best. Twenty-five years later, in 1938, the captain's findings were confirmed by another German, Dr. Leo von Boxberger. He was a magistrate who had spent many years working in the Cameroons. "The belief in a gigantic water-animal," he wrote, "described as a reptile with a long thin neck, exists among the natives throughout the Southern Cameroons wherever they form part of the Congo basin, and also to the west of this area . . . wherever the great rivers are broad and deep and are flanked by virgin forest."

However, neither man was the first European to have experiences of monsters on the so-called Dark Continent. This distinction probably lies with two others of their countrymen, Carl Hagenbeck and Hans Schomburgk. Their adventure took place in 1909.

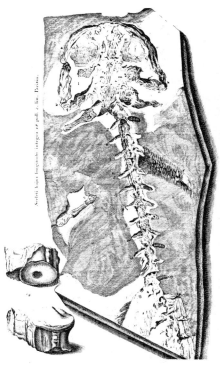

Hagenbeck and Schomburgk were two renowned wild animal dealers. For years they had heard identical stories from locals and travelers about the existence of what Hagenbeck in his book *Beasts and Man* called "an immense and wholly unknown animal." Known as the King of the Zoos because of his work in supplying wild animals, Hagenbeck was fascinated by the creature reported to be half dragon and half elephant. It was said to have a single horn like the rhinoceros, but as Dr. Heuvelmans later points out, "an animal may look like a rhinoceros without being one." Hagenbeck believed the beast to be a dinosaur, one that was "seemingly akin to the brontosaurus." At "great expense" he later sent out an expedition to

Above: how the earth must have trembled in those far-off times when monstrously huge dinosaurs battled each other! Here is what the scene might have looked like in an attack by *Tyrannosaurus rex*, largest biped dinosaur that ever lived, on the immense but weaker duck-billed *Trachodon*. Left: our knowledge of dinosaurs is comparatively new. For many centuries men took no particular note of fossil bones uncovered, or decided that they belonged to human giants. These bones of an *ichthyosaurus* were explained learnedly in 1726 as the bones of one of the vast numbers of people drowned in the biblical flood. Right: a 19th-century expedition collects dinosaur bones for the American professor Othniel Charles Marsh, one of the first scientists to study dinosaurs by using uncovered fossil material.

Above: drawing of a *Triceratops*, a three-horned dinosaur. When a Belgian named Lepage, reported being chased by a horned monster in Africa in 1919, the well-known naturalist Bernard Heuvelmans said that the animal described most resembled the *Triceratops*.

Below: the German wild game dealer Carl Hagenbeck. From his experiences in Africa at the turn of this century, he was convinced that a dinosaur-like reptile still existed in the jungle swamplands.

find the beast. Unfortunately, the party was forced to return without having discovered any evidence for or against the monster's presence.

It was not until ten years later—and after Captain von Stein had written his report—that the monsters of central Africa again made news. In the London *Times* of November 17, 1919, a story stated that an "extraordinary monster" had been encountered in what was then the Belgian Congo. In October it had charged a Monsieur Lepage, who was in charge of railway construction in the area. Lepage fired on the beast, and then fled with the creature in full pursuit. Only when the animal tired and gave up the chase was he able to examine it through his binoculars. The animal, he told *The Times* correspondent in Port Elizabeth, was some "24 feet in length with a long pointed snout adorned with tusks like horns and a short horn above the nostrils. The front feet were like those of a horse, and the hind hoofs were cloven. There was a scaly lump on the monster's shoulder."

Soon afterward the animal—by then said to be a dinosaur— rampaged through a nearby village, killing some of the inhabitants. Despite this, the Belgian government prohibited anyone from hurting or molesting the beast. Officials told a hunt that was organized that the animal was "probably a relic of antiquity," and therefore must not be harmed. "There is," added *The Times,* "a wild trackless region in the neighborhood which contains many swamps and marshes, where, says the head of the [local] museum, it is possible that a few primeval monsters may survive."

The Times account made a particular impression on Captain Leicester Stevens, who was even more excited when on December

FEET   5   10   15   20   25   30   35

W. Winans
Dec 12, 1919

Above: a sketch by big game hunter Walter Winans of the *bronto-saurus* he claimed had been described to him by Carl Hagenbeck. Dr. Heuvelmans said that it was completely unlike a true *brontosaurus*, calling it the "mongrel offspring of a lion and a medieval dragon."

Below: a true *brontosaurus*, which was a herbivorous dinosaur up to 60 feet long. Bones have been found in the western United States.

4 he read a report from Africa that the monster had been seen in another part of the Congo. This time the beast, said to be a brontosaurus, had been trailed by a Belgian big game hunter. He had followed the "strange spoor" for some 12 miles, and had then come across an animal "certainly of the rhinoceros order with large scales reaching far down its body." He fired at the monster, which then threw its head up and lumbered off into a swamp. "The American Smithsonian expedition," the report ended, "was in search of the monster . . . when it met with a serious railway accident in which several persons were killed."

After the fatal accident, the Smithsonian Institution offered a $3 million reward for the monster, dead or alive. On learning this, Captain Stevens decided that he would hunt the dinosaur down. With his mongrel dog Laddie, which was part wolf, he set out by train from London's Waterloo Station on the first stage of his journey to central Africa. Laddie, a "barrage dog" which had been used as a front line message carrier in France in 1914–18, was prepared, according to Stevens, to take on anything from a tank to a dinosaur. "I am leaving for Cape Town on Christmas Eve," the captain told a newspaper reporter on the train. "From Cape Town I shall go 1700 miles north to Kafue, where my expedition will be organized."

Armed with a Mannlicher rifle, Captain Stevens claimed that he knew the location of a "vital spot" on the monster, which was

93

Above: *Steneosaurus bollensis*, one of the first true crocodiles. It appeared on earth in the early Jurassic period over 150 million years ago. It was one of the commonest, and grew to between 13 and 20 feet. Dr. A. Monard, who investigated the African stories of the *lipata*, a gigantic amphibian, concluded that it was a species of crocodile and not a prehistoric animal of any kind.

especially vulnerable to bullets. "Where that spot is," he said mysteriously, "is one of my secrets." His venture fired the imagination of both the general public and expert animal hunters. One of the latter, the American Walter Winans, supplied the London *Daily Mail* with a picture he claimed to have taken of a brontosaurus in the central African swamps. This was followed by a letter to the paper from another experienced big game hunter, R. G. Burton, in which he advised Captain Stevens to take a "more effective battery of guns" with him.

"If the animal is anything like the monster conjured up by Mr. Walter Winans," he wrote, "the hunter had better take a tank instead of his 'barrage dog.' To receive the charge of 80 feet of primeval monster, armor-plated and exuding poison from fangs and skin . . . Mannlicher and repeating Winchester rifles are quite inadequate. I would be sorry to face even a charging tiger with such weapons, while the shotgun, unless it is for the purpose of scattering salt on the tail of the creature, will prove worse than useless. He should take nothing less than a field gun— say an 18 pounder. Armed with a tank, with heavy artillery and with a supply of poison gas, the modern St. George might make 'merry music' against this 'dragon of the prime,' and have a fair chance of taking the £1 million offered by the Smithsonian Institution when he comes galumphing back with the skin."

It would appear that Burton's warning was a sound one. A single report came out that Captain Stevens had encountered his monster "crashing through the reeds of a swamp, and that it was the brontosaurus—a huge marsh animal, ten times as big as the biggest elephant." Nothing more was publicly heard of the hunter. The Smithsonian's reward went unclaimed, and in February 1920, a member of the Institution's expedition dismissed the monster stories as a practical joke. Whether or not this was true, there was no denying the fact that, from then on, the search for and sighting of dinosaurs was to be a regular feature of the central African scene.

One of the most dramatic dinosaur sightings took place 12 years later in February 1932. J. C. Johanson, a Swedish rubber plantation overseer, was out on a shooting trip in the Kasai valley when he and his African servant suddenly saw an incredible sight—a 16-yard-long monster with the head and tail of a lizard. The beast disappeared almost at once, but reappeared again in a large swamp that the two men had to cross to get home. Just 25 yards separated the hunters and the creature. The African fled. Johanson fainted, but just before he passed out, he managed to put his camera to use. The experience left the overseer ill for eight days.

The photographs taken by Johanson were later printed in Germany in the *Cologne Gazette,* and this was reported in the *Rhodesia Herald.* "The photos," the newspaper story went, " . . . were anything but clear, yet they revealed a discovery of great importance. Johanson stumbled on a unique specimen of a dinosaur family that must have lived milleniums ago." It was similar to an outsized lizard seen a few months later in the summer of 1932 by a young South African hunter. Even so, accusations of fake were once again made. Support for the possibility of such sightings came from the Swiss zoologist Dr. A.

Monard who, also in 1932, accompanied a dinosaur expedition to Angola.

"The existence of a large saurian descended from the reptiles of the Mesozoic era [the third major geological era] is by no means theoretically impossible," he wrote in a Swiss scientific journal. "Though every continent has been crossed and re-crossed, most travelers follow much the same track, and there are still holes in the net to be explored. There have been several reports that some kind of 'brontosaurus' survives, and several expeditions have even gone to look for it; the fact that they failed may merely prove that this prehistoric beast is very rare or that it lives in country as inaccessible as the great swamps are. There are some reasons, based on the history of the continents and of the great reptiles, for thinking that they could survive . . . While it is not scientific to be too credulous, it is no better to be in-credulous; and there is no reason for saying that the survival of some types of Mesozoic saurians is impossible."

Dr. Monard's optimism, however, was not borne out when he and his companions reached Angola later that year. They were hoping to find a *lipata*, an enormous and "very voracious" amphibian. It was much larger and fiercer than a crocodile, and was only seen at the end of the rainy season from July to Sep-tember. In spite of paddling for days through the marshes in the sun and rain to follow up every lead, the animal was not found.

Seven years afterward Mrs. Ilse von Nolde, who had lived in eastern Angola for 10 years, had better luck. She actually heard the "water-lion" roaring at night, and knew that the local hippopotami fled the district whenever they heard the fearsome sounds. "All the people dwelling along the tributaries of the

Above: a *Stegosaurus*. This pre-historic animal most nearly fits the description of the fearsome *row* which the explorer Charles Miller claimed to have seen and photographed while in New Guinea. Below: jacket of Miller's book published in 1950. The photo-graph of the row was not in it.

Left: Professor J. C. B. Smith, South Africa's best-known expert on fish, with the second coelacanth discovered in 1952. In 1938 Smith had seen the first one ever found only after it had decayed badly. He then put out a leaflet offering a reward for the fish, but had to wait 14 years until the next one was brought to him.

Below: scientists examining a coelacanth in a cold store. Since 1952 close to 100 more have been caught, but none has lived in captivity longer than a few hours.

Above: a coelacanth, living link with the unknown and far distant past. When the first of these big prehistoric fishes was caught, startled fishermen could not get near it because of its vicious snapping. It died in three hours.

Kuango know about the 'water-lion,'" she wrote in an article published in a German colonial gazette. "They had heard it roar during the night, but none of them has ever seen one—at least none of those I talked to—and they say it will come ashore during the night only, and hide in the water during the day."

After this partial anticlimax in 1939, the next decade was mostly taken up with stories and articles about World War II and its aftermath. It wasn't until the publication in London in 1950 of explorer Charles Miller's book *Cannibal Caravan* that the monsters of the unknown made news again. The material for the book had been gathered when Miller and his society bride had spent their honeymoon among the head-hunting cannibals of New Guinea. There they heard of a 40-foot-long lizard known among local people as *row*, because of the noise it made. The beast lived on the top of a high grassy plateau, and the couple decided to make their way up and take pictures of the animal. They reached the summit and looked over the edge of a cliff, where they saw a large triangular-shaped marsh. As they gazed, the reeds below them began to stir, and a long yellowy-brown neck swayed up toward the sky. Miller froze on the spot and his wife, who came over to join him, fell to the grass and lay there too scared to lift her head. Then Miller pointed his camera at the creature.

"As if in obedience to my wishes," he wrote, "the colossal remnant of the age of dinosaurs stalked across the swamp. Once its tail lashed out of the grass so far behind its head I thought it must be another beast. For one brief second I saw the horny point.

I heard it hiss—roooow, roooow, roooow . . . It was a full quarter mile away, it couldn't possibly hear the camera, but I found myself cowering back as if that snapping turtle-shaped beak would lash out and nab me. I gasped with relief when the creature settled back . . . Twice more the row reared up, giving me a good view of the bony flange around its head and the projecting plates along its backbone. Then with a click my camera ran out just as the row slithered behind a growth of dwarf eucalyptus."

Miller's book had numerous illustrations, but there was none of the row that had so frightened him and his wife. He offered his dinosaur film to several producers, but it was never commercially shown. However, as Dr. Heuvelmans stresses in his retelling of Miller's adventure, "it would be rash to assert that such an animal is impossible—zoology and paleontology [the study of fossils] are full of surprises . . ."

Despite this further disappointment, professional and amateur monster lovers refuse to believe that such creatures do not exist except in controversial books. Ivan Sanderson, who had first-hand experience of a monster in Africa, asserts that much of our present-day world is unknown, and he attacks the popular notion that there is little left to be fully explored and mapped. "There was never a greater misconception," he writes. "The percentage of the land surface of the earth that is actually inhabited—that is to say, lived upon, enclosed, farmed, or regularly traversed—is quite limited. Even if the territory that is penetrated only for hunting or the gathering of food crops be added, vast areas still remain completely unused. There are such areas in every continent, areas that for years are never even entered by man. Nor are these only the hot deserts of the torrid regions or the cold deserts of the poles . . . There might easily be creatures as big as elephants living in some profusion in, say, the back of the Guyanas, which are now only a few hours' flight in a commercial plane from Miami. Such animals might have been well-known to several thousand people for hundreds of years, but their presence would still be unsuspected by us, for few of the Amerindians—who from aerial surveys are known to exist in that area—have ever come out, or even been seen by anyone from outside."

That creatures we call monsters exist somewhere today is not totally impossible. This was demonstrated in 1938 with the discovery off the coast of South Africa of a live coelacanth—a huge fish dating from millions of years ago, and naturally assumed to be extinct long since. The fossils of other coelacanths showed the species to be some 70 million years old. Scientists were further amazed and delighted when, in 1952, a second live coelacanth was caught off Madagascar. Since then close to 100 more of these hardy survivors from the past have been discovered and studied, although most live for only a few hours in captivity. Their home is in the Indian Ocean near the Comore Islands. These discoveries now make it logical to ask: "If prehistoric coelacanths are still living today, why not dinosaurs?"

It is possible that dinosaurs exist in spite of all the doubters, and, like the coelacanth, are a link in the long chain of living beings. But, unlike the fish, they are savage, huge, lumbering monstrosities not so easily captured.

Mammoths in the Siberian Forest

A Russian hunter in 1918 was exploring the taiga—the vast forest that covers nearly three million square miles of Siberia —when he encountered huge tracks in thick layers of mud by a lake in a clearing. They were about 2 feet across and about 18 inches long, and appeared to be oval. The creature was obviously four-footed, and had wandered into the woods. The hunter followed the tracks curiously, from time to time finding huge heaps of dung apparently composed of vegetable matter. The tree branches were broken off about 10 feet up, as if the animal's enormous head had forced its way through. For days he followed the tracks. Then he saw traces of a second animal, and a trampling of the tracks, as if the two creatures had been excited by the meeting. Then the two went on together.

The hunter followed. Suddenly, one afternoon, he saw them. They were enormous hairy elephants with great white tusks curved upward. The hair was a dark chestnut color, very heavy on the hindquarters, but lighter toward the front. The beasts moved very slowly.

The last of the mammoths are believed to have died more than 12,000 years ago, and the hunter knew nothing about them. But did he see one?

6

The Abominable Snowman

It was around teatime on a cold November afternoon in 1951. British mountaineers Eric Shipton and Michael Ward, returning from the Everest Reconnaissance Expedition, were making their way over the Menlung Glacier some 20,000 feet above sea level between Tibet and Nepal. Suddenly they came across a giant footprint in the snow. It measured 13 by 18 inches! As they saw it, the two men stopped and stared at each other. They knew the imprint had been recently made because it had not had time to melt. This meant that it was closer to actual size than a melted print, which appears larger. Therefore its size was the more

In the icy silent mountains of the Himalayas, it seems curious enough to find any animal life at all. But to find traces of giant two-legged creatures apparently making their home in eternal snow! Mountaineers came down from the heights with tales of the Yeti, and the public imagination was swiftly captured.

Above: a magazine illustration for a fictional surprise encounter of an armed man with the Snowman, a musk ox lurking behind him.

Right: mysterious tracks seen and photographed by climber Don Whillans in 1970 during an assault on the south face of Annapurna. That night he saw an apelike creature in bright moonlight bounding along the ridge above. He didn't see it again after that.

"Several sets of inexplicable tracks"

amazing. Had the footmark been made by a giant human or a huge snow monster? As they speculated, and before they could recover from their initial surprise, they noticed a set of fresh looking tracks in the deep snow lining the lip of the glacier. Almost too excited to speak, they followed the trail for nearly a mile before the snow became thinner and the tracks disappeared. The two seasoned mountain climbers realized that they could be on the verge of a major anthropological discovery, and quickly set about taking photographs of their find.

Using Ward's ice axe and snowboots to show scale, Shipton took two photographs in which the footprints were well defined and perfectly in focus. These photographs were to cause controversy, doubt, and sometimes downright disbelief in every country in which they were later reproduced. Despite those who called the photographs everything short of fake, there was no disputing the fact that the prints had not been made by monkeys, bears, leopards, or ordinary human beings. In that case, then, what kind of creature had preceded the explorers across that remote section of the Himalayas? Whatever it was, it had five distinct toes with the inner two toes larger than the rest, the smaller toes pressed together, and the heel flat and exceptionally broad. If Eric Shipton was in any doubt at the time he photographed the footmarks in 1951, he had certainly made his mind up 10 years later. In a foreword to Odette Tchernine's book *The Snowman and Company* he wrote:

"Before 1951, though like other travelers I had seen several sets of inexplicable tracks in the snows of the Himalayas and Karakoram, and had listened to innumerable stories of the 'Yeti' told by my Sherpa friends, I was inclined to dismiss the creature as fantasy. But the tracks which Michael Ward . . . and I found in the Menlung Basin after the Everest Reconnaissance Expedition, were so fresh and showed so clearly the outline and contours of the naked feet that I could no longer remain a skeptic. There could be no doubt whatever that a large creature had passed that way a very short time before, and that whatever it was it was not a human being, not a bear, not any species of monkey known to exist in Asia."

The newspapers of the day—and indeed those since then—seized upon the story as eagerly as they had earlier publicized the newsworthy Loch Ness Monster. Playing down the Tibetan name Yeti—meaning "magical creature"—they popularized the name "Abominable Snowman"—which got across the idea of horror associated with the being that was said to exist in the valleys, gaps, and glaciers of the Himalayas. The London Zoological Society and the Natural History department of the British Museum examined the photographs and came to the conclusion that the prints had been caused by a langur monkey or a red bear. The creature's stride alone—a length of some $2\frac{1}{2}$ feet—made nonsense of the monkey theory. But these austere authorities remained unconvinced, and it was left to the highly regarded British medical journal *The Lancet* to give credence to Shipton's Abominable Snowman claims. In an article published in June 1960, and headed "Giants with Cold Feet," it stated:

"Even in the 20th century there are many thinly populated and almost unexplored regions of the world, and in several of these

Above: Eric Shipton, the British mountain climber who is a veteran of expeditions on Mt. Everest. He and Michael Ward encountered peculiar and unfamiliar giant footprints during the Everest Reconnaissance Expedition of 1951, and photographed them. This fed the controversy about the Yeti.

Below: the giant footprints that Shipton, Ward, and their guide Sen Tensing discovered near the Menlung Glacier. Ward's ice axe is laid by the footprint to show the scale. Ward said that they followed the track for about half a mile. Where the animal had crossed a small crevasse it was possible to see how its toes had dug in to get a firm hold. It even appeared that there might be an imprint of the nails, but it wasn't possible to be sure.

there have arisen rumors of the existence of large animals still awaiting scientific discovery and classification. The publicity accorded to the 'Abominable Snowman' of the Himalayas is no doubt a tribute to the aura of mystery and endeavor surrounding the highest mountain on earth. It may also be due in part to the beguiling name bestowed upon the creature, almost certainly as a result of a losing battle with the local dialect.''

Although the Yeti was big news in the 1950s and early 1960s, it was already old news, with sightings dating back to 1832. According to the well-known anatomist and anthropologist Dr. John Napier, the source of the Abominable Snowman stories were the "military and Civil Service pioneers in the last century, and the high mountaineers in this." Because of them, Napier says,

Above: how myths are made. These cloven-hoofed prints were long accepted as a Yeti trail simply because they were photographed on the same day and in the same area as the Shipton-Ward ones, and so filed together in the Mt. Everest Expedition archives. They are clearly goat footprints.

"the eastern Himalayas are better known than most of the other mountain ranges where monster myths are prevalent."

It was in 1832 that B. H. Hodgson, the British Resident in Nepal, published an article about a strange mountain creature in a scientific journal. He wrote that some Nepalese porters of his had "fled in terror" from an erect, tailless being with shaggy black hair that had ambled up to them. They called the creature a *rakshas*, the Sanskrit word for "demon," and informed him that references to such wild men went back to the 4th century B.C. In those early times, rakshas appeared in the Indian national epic *Rama and Sita*. Hodgson derided his servants' talk of a demon creature, and explained the intruder away as a stray orang-utan. Fifty-seven years later, however, in 1889, Major L. A. Waddell of the Indian Army Medical Corps became the first European to see footprints presumably made by one of the mountain monsters. He discovered the tracks 17,000 feet up in northeast Sikkim, but was reluctant to ascribe them to the then unnamed Snowman. In his book *Among the Himalayas*, he stated:

"The belief in these creatures is universal among Tibetans. None, however, of the Tibetans I have interrogated on the subject could ever give me an authentic case. On the most superficial investigation it always resolved into something that somebody had heard tell of." In his conclusion, Waddell insisted that the "so-called hairy wild men" were simply vicious, meat-eating yellow snow bears that frequently preyed upon yaks.

The next recorded sighting of tracks by a European came in 1914 when J. R. P. Gent, a British forestry officer stationed in Sikkim, wrote of discovering footprints of what must have been a huge and amazing creature. "The peculiar feature," he said, "is that its tracks are about 18–24 inches long, and the toes point in the opposite direction to that in which the animal is moving . . . I take it that he walks on his knees and shins instead of on the sole of his foot."

It was only a matter of time before the inevitable encounter between a European and a mysterious Yeti. It came in 1921 when Lieutenant-Colonel C. K. Howard-Bury led the first Everest Reconnaissance Expedition. He and his team were clambering over a ridge some 21,000 feet up. Suddenly one of his Sherpa guides gripped his arm excitedly and pointed to a dark upright figure moving rapidly through the snow. The Sherpas immediately jumped to the conclusion that this must be "the wild man of the snows." On his return to his own country, Howard-Bury read up on the ways and customs of the Himalaya wild man. He learned that naughty little Tibetan children are threatened into good behavior by warnings about him. "To escape from him they must run down the hill, as then his long hair falls over his eyes and he is unable to see them," Howard-Bury said.

There is also a female of the species, and the Sherpas say that Yeti women are hampered by the size of their breasts. One investigator of the creatures was told by a Sherpa, "We followed the track of two Yeti, they were both females—their breasts were so large they have to throw them over their shoulders before they bend down."

In the spring of 1925 a sighting was made by the British photographer N. A. Tombazi. He observed one of the elusive

Above: the vast trackless wastes
of the high Himalayan mountains.
This view is from the Western
Cwm on the shoulder of Mt.
Everest, looking at the giant
peak of Pumori, 23,442 feet high.

Left: the chief lama of Khumjung
with the scalp thought to be
that of a Snowman. It is kept
as a relic in the monastery.

Right: lamas perform a ceremonial
dance to invoke certain deities.
The religious and mythological
content of Tibetan Buddhism is
filled with demons, spirits, and
other strange beings. Therefore
it is natural for the people of the
high mountains to believe in the
Yeti as a supernatural creature.

Left: the only tangible evidence of the existence of the Yeti is the scalps treasured by various monasteries. This one comes from Pangboche on the trial to Mount Everest, so has been frequently reported by outsiders. There have been stories of Yeti skins, but so far there are no photographs. Sherpa porters have often said that tracks encountered by an expedition were Yeti tracks, but one authority reminds us that the Sherpas consider it highly ill-mannered to disappoint anyone.

Above: the Khumjung Yeti scalp, which is hundreds of years old. When it was brought to the West, Dr. Heuvelmans was one of the scientists who studied it. Without denying the existence of the Yeti, he said the scalp was a fake made from a mountain goat's. He explained that it was probably made long ago as a dance mask.

beings 15,000 feet up the Zemu Glacier and, as a Fellow of the Royal Geographical Society, his testimony was not to be laughed aside. Again it was a Sherpa who drew attention to the Snowman's presence, but to begin with the bright glare of the snow prevented the photographer from seeing the newcomer. Then, as his eyes grew accustomed to the dazzle, he spotted the creature some 200 or 300 yards away in a valley to the east of the camp. In his book *Bigfoot* John Napier quotes the photographer as follows:

"Unquestionably the figure in outline was exactly like a human being, walking upright and stopping occasionally to uproot or pull at some dwarf rhododendron bushes. It showed up dark against the snow and, as far as I could make out, wore no clothes. Within the next minute or so it had moved into some thick scrub and was lost to view. Such a fleeting glimpse, unfortunately, did not allow me to set the telephoto-camera, or even to fix the object carefully with the binoculars; but a couple of hours later, during the descent, I purposely made a detour so as to pass the place where the 'man' or 'beast' had been seen. I examined the footprints which were clearly visible on the surface of the snow. They were similar in shape to those of a man . . . The prints were undoubtedly biped, the order of the spoor having no characteristics whatever of any imaginable quadruped. From enquiries I made a few days later at Yokson, on my return journey, I gathered that no man had gone in [that] direction since the beginning of the year."

By now belief in the Yeti was growing from country to

country, and reports of the creature's habits and behavior were coming from men of prominence and responsibility. The English mountaineer Maurice Wilson, who died in 1934 while attempting to climb Everest alone, was convinced that the Snowmen existed, and that they were mystical hermits rather than wild beasts. This theory was shared by the German missionary-doctor, Father Franz Eichinger. He told the London *News Chronicle* that the Yeti were solitary monks who had withdrawn from the pressures of civilization, and who lived in cold but contemplative peace in their mountain caves. In 1938 the Yeti emerged as creatures of kindness and sympathy according to the story of Captain d'Auvergne, the curator of the Victoria Memorial near Chowringhee in Calcutta. Injured while traveling on his own in the Himalayas, and threatened with snowblindness and exposure, he was saved from death by a 9-foot-tall Yeti. The giant picked him up, carried him several miles to a cave, and fed and nursed him until he was able to make his way back home. Captain d'Auvergne concluded that his savior was a survivor from some prehistoric human tribe or sect. Like Father Eichinger, he believed that the Snowman and his fellows belonged to an ancient people called the A–o–re who had fled to the mountains to avoid persecution, and who then developed into beastlike giants.

All this was sensational enough, but an even more vivid, explicit, and dramatic encounter was to take place. It occurred in February 1942, but was not made public until the following decade when Slavomir Rawicz's best-selling book *The Long Walk* appeared. In it Rawicz, a Pole, tells how he and six friends escaped from a Siberian prisoner of war camp, and crossed the Himalayas to freedom in India. The book came under widespread attack as being more fiction than fact, many critics citing the physical unlikelihood of weakened escapees being able to make such a journey—which included a 12-day hike across the Gobi desert with little food and no water. There was also extreme skepticism about Rawicz's story of meeting two 8-foot tall creatures somewhere between Bhutan and Sikkim. For two hours, according to the author, he and his companions watched the outsize animals or men from a distance of 100 yards. He gauged the monster's height by using his military training for artillery observations.

In 1953 the Yeti again made international news when New Zealander Edmund Hillary and Sherpa Tenzing Norgay spotted giant prints during their conquest of Mt. Everest. In some quarters their feat was practically eclipsed by their discovery of the Yeti footmarks. Such prints were a familiar sight to Tenzing, who had grown up in a village on the Khumbu Glacier, and who told Hillary that his father—"who was no teller of lies"—had once almost been killed by one of the Snowmen. The older Tenzing had come across the creature while it was eating, and had been chased by it down a steep slope. He escaped by running downhill "for his life."

It was such anecdotes that led the London *Daily Mail* to organize its own Abominable Snowman Expedition in 1954. Two years before, Yeti tracks had also been seen by Dr. Eduard Wyse-Dunant, the leader of a Swiss Everest Expedition.

They Saw the Abominable Snowman

In the decade after World War II Slavomir Rawicz, a Polish refugee living in England, wrote about his experiences in *The Long Walk*. In this book he claimed that he and six others escaped from a Siberian prison camp and walked 2000 miles to freedom. During their grueling journey to India they crossed the Himalayas. It was there, one day in May 1942, that he said they saw two massive Yeti.

"They were nearly eight feet tall and standing erect," Rawicz wrote. "The heads were squarish and . . . the shoulders sloped sharply down to a powerful chest and long arms, the wrists of which reached the knees." One was slightly larger than the other, and Rawicz and his companions concluded they were a male and female. The unknown creatures looked at the humans, but appeared completely indifferent. Unfortunately, they were in the middle of the most obvious route for the refugees to continue their descent, and the men were disinclined to approach much closer in spite of the apparent lack of interest.

The refugee party finally moved off by another route. Behind them the Yeti watched their retreat with obvious unconcern, and then turned away to look out over the magnificent scenery.

Above: Tenzing Norgay on the summit of Mount Everest, photographed by Edmund Hillary. It was on this climb to the top that the pair saw footprints which Tensing identified as those of a Yeti. Hillary was intrigued enough to mount an expedition later to investigate the existence of the Yeti, although the expedition also intended to find out about the adaptation of the human body to the effects of high altitudes.

Because he found "no trace of meals, nor yet of excrement," Dr. Wyse-Dunant believed that the "animal is only passing through and does not frequent these heights." His view was confirmed by the experience of the *Daily Mail* team, which came up with nothing more positive than a few hairs from a 300-year-old alleged Yeti scalp kept in a Buddhist temple. This scalp, conical in shape, was about 8 inches high and had a base circumference of 26 inches. It was photographed by *Mail* journalist Ralph Izzard, who later had the hairs analyzed. He was told they belonged to "no known animal."

In his book about the expedition, *The Abominable Snowman Adventure,* Izzard asserted that their effort, though a stunt to boost circulation, had not been worthless. "I am personally convinced," he wrote, "that sooner or later the Yeti will be found, and that it will be sooner rather than later because of our efforts. One must, however, add a word of warning to future expeditions. I think it is the opinion of all of us when we review our own experiences that the Yeti is more likely to be met in a chance encounter round say, a rock, than by an organized search . . . In such country there is no question of stalking an animal in the accepted sense of the term. For miles at a time there may be only one safe path used by men and animals alike, for to deviate from it would mean taking unacceptable risks from crevasses, avalanches, and other hazards. Often such a path . . . may cross the dead center of a snowfield where a party is as conspicuous as a line of black beetles on a white tablecloth and where, from the surrounding cliffs, a lurking animal can hold one under observation for hours at a time with freedom of choice to lie low or steal away across the next horizon . . . That we failed to see a Yeti signified nothing, either for or against its existence . . . There are, I know, many who rejoice that we failed in our main objective—that a last great mystery remains in this much picked-over world to challenge adventurous spirits."

Just as Izzard had observed, the "great mystery" inspired three American safaris in 1957, 1958 and 1959. They were financed and headed by the tycoons Tom Slick and F. Kirk Johnson. The expeditions carried hypodermic rifles and bullets, which the Yeti wisely stayed miles away from, and the nearest the well-equipped parties came to success was when the two millionaires took some excellent plaster casts of Yeti prints. Other well-substantiated reports of sightings continued to appear in books and interviews. Mountaineer John Hunt, in his account of the 1953 scaling of Everest, told about a story he heard from the dignified Abbot of Thyangboche Monastery. It seems that a few winters previously, the religious leader had seen a Yeti. Hunt reports the Abbot's story as follows:

"This beast, loping along sometimes on his hind legs and sometimes on all fours, stood about five feet high and was covered with gray hair . . . The Yeti had stopped to scratch . . . had picked up snow, played with it, and made a few grunts . . . instructions were given to drive off the unwelcome visitor. Conch shells were blown, and the long traditional horns sounded. The Yeti had ambled away into the bush."

During the 1950s several Soviet scientists took the Yeti seriously. Dr. A. G. Pronin, a hydrologist at Leningrad Uni-

versity, for instance, sighted one of the creatures in 1958 in the Pamir Mountains in Central Asia, and was duly impressed. Odette Tchernine gives an account of Pronin's encounter in her book *The Yeti*. "At first glance," he wrote, "I took it to be a bear, but then I saw it more clearly, and realized that it was a manlike creature. It was walking on two feet, upright, but in a stooping fashion. It was quite naked, and its thickset body was covered with reddish hair. The arms were overlong, and swung slightly with each movement. I watched it for about ten minutes before it disappeared, very swiftly, among the scrub and boulders."

Despite being attacked in some newspapers, the doctor's story was listened to in official circles. As a result, a professor of Historical Science, Dr. Boris Porshnev, was appointed head of a Commission for Studying the Question of the Abominable Snowman. His on-the-spot investigations convinced him that the Yeti was not just another traveler's tale, but actually existed. "In the 15th century such wild people lived in the mountain fastnesses near the Gobi desert," he stated. "They had no permanent homes. Their bodies, except for hands and faces, were covered with hair. Like animals they fed on leaves, grass, and anything they could find." A third Soviet authority who refused to discount the Snowman was Professor Stanyukovich. Around 1960, he went to the Pamirs with a Yeti expedition that included some of his country's most expert zoologists, archeologists, botanists, and climbers. After nine months of patient endeavor, during which cameras with telescopic lenses were at the ready in concealed observation posts, the creatures had still not been seen—either in person or by way of footprints. The Yeti had prudently ignored the 20 goats and rams put out as bait, and avoided the dozens of snares, nets, and the team of snow-

Above: Edmund Hillary before the 1960–61 Yeti expedition. He shows newsmen a drawing of the Abominable Snowman based on the reports of several witnesses who claimed to have seen the elusive mountain monster. Ward, who had seen the footprints with Shipton, was an expedition member. Below: Hillary with the Khumjung Yeti scalp that he brought back, and Khumbo Chumbi, the Sherpa assigned as caretaker of the scalp.

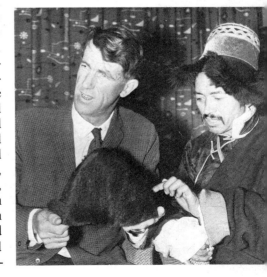

leopard hunters who spent more than three months lying in cunningly hidden dugouts.

The professor took it philosophically, however. "Farewell, you fascinating riddle," he wrote. "Farewell, inscrutable Snowman, ruler of the heights and snows. A pity, a thousand pities that you are not to be found. What, not at all? Not anywhere? Perhaps you are yet to be found in the remotest mountains of Nepal. Perhaps!"

Edmund Hillary led his own commercially backed Yeti expedition in 1960–61. Although he returned with a Snowman scalp lent to him by the Khumjung monastery, the Yeti remained as evasive as ever. Zoologists classified the scalp as that of a serow, or goat antelope, which is a native of eastern Asia—and only some unfamiliar parasites found among the hair were new to them. At this time, information about the Abominable Snowman had been systematized, and it had become clear that there are three distinct types: the *Rimi*, which can be up to 8 feet tall and dwells at the comparatively low level of 8000 feet; the *Nyalmot*, an improbable 15 feet in height and a meat eater that feeds on mountain goats and yak; and the *Rakshi-Bompo*, a mere 5 feet in stature and a vegetarian that lives on grain and millet. A shy and retiring being, the Yeti of all three types prefers to come out at night, and is rarely seen in more than twos. It also appreciates it if bowls of water and food are left where it can find them. The Nepalese and Tibetans will not kill or harm the beast in the belief that to do so will result in bad luck and general misfortune. The creature is usually described as having long reddish hair and feet that, according to the Sherpas, are placed back to front. They get this idea from its prints, which appear to be going in a contrary direction.

The Yeti is reputed to have a body odor that makes a skunk smell good, and to possess such strength that it can throw boulders around as if they were marbles and uproot trees as if they were flowers. Descriptions of the Yeti's voice range from shrill whistles to high-pitched yelps to lion-throated roars. It is also said to be fond of any kind of alcohol.

As more evidence about the Yeti piled up, the Nepal government took a definite stand in 1961. The Yeti, it claimed, positively existed, and was to be found in an S-shaped area incorporating Siberia and Southeastern USSR, India, Alaska, Canada, and the USA. Therefore, the Nepalese granted licenses at a cost of $10,000 to hunters dedicated and rich enough to stalk the beast through the Himalayas. Special triangular stamps were issued by the enterprising Bhutanese Post Office, which depicted the Snowman as a being peculiar to the mountains of Bhutan.

Some experts believe not only that the Yeti exists, but also that it will sooner or later be caught and brought down to civilization—and, presumably, to a caged life in one of the world's leading zoos. The latest theory about the Snowman's origins comes from a team of three zoologists who, toward the end of 1972, set out to hunt the fabled beast. They believe that the Yeti may be a descendant of the giant ape *Gigantopithecus*, which 500,000 years ago retreated to the mountains of southern Asia. At that time the Himalayas were rising by as much as 2400 to 3000 meters. Because of this increase in the height of the mountains, the

Above: Texas oilman Tom Slick, bandaged from a truck accident on the approach to the mountains. He had financed three attempts to find the Snowman. Slick said he was almost convinced of the Snowman's existence when he photographed Yeti tracks and collected a few wisps of hair that he brought back for analysis.

Above: the London *Daily Mail* Yeti team of the 1954 Himalayan Expedition, photographed at base camp with the expedition Sherpas.
Above right: Sherpa Ang Tschering pointing to a line of Yeti tracks that ran alongside the tracks made by the expedition. This was as close to a Yeti as the expedition managed to get.
Right: the Russian historian Boris Porshnev, a scholar of wide learning who holds doctorates in historical and philosophical sciences. He is convinced that the Yeti exists and that it will so be proved one day. He believes that the best approach would be not to capture the Snowman, but to make contact with it and attempt to get it semi-domesticated. Then a Yeti Reserve should be set up to protect the creature and allow full scientific research to proceed.
Below right: Don Whillans, who made the most recent sighting of the mysterious Snowman on the Annapurna expedition in March 1970.

Snowman may have become isolated. The zoologists' idea was to seek the Yeti in the forests of Katmandu, rather than at higher altitudes. They have not yet revealed anything about their mission, so the most recent recorded sighting of the Abominable Snowman remains the one reported in March 1970. It was then that Don Whillans, deputy leader of the triumphant British Annapurna Expedition, discovered and photographed Yeti footprints in the Machapuchare region of Nepal—and, by the light of the moon, saw a Yetilike being "bounding along on all fours."

In his best-selling book *Annapurna South Face*, team leader Chris Bonnington quotes Whillans as saying: "The following morning I went up to make a full reconnaissance to the permanent Base Camp site, and I took the two Sherpas along. I thought I'd see their reaction at the point where I'd photographed the tracks the day before. The tracks were so obvious that it was impossible not to make any comment, but they walked straight past and didn't indicate that they had seen them. I had already mentioned that I had seen the Yeti, not knowing exactly what it was, but they pretended they didn't understand and ignored what I said. I am convinced that they believe the Yeti does exist, that it is some kind of sacred animal which is best left alone; that if you don't bother it, it won't bother you."

Whillans also had the British Medical Association magazine *The Lancet* on his side, for in a 1960 article the journal concluded: "Now that the Himalayas are more frequented by mountaineers than formerly, information is likely to accumulate more rapidly,

Below: whether it exists or not, the Yeti goes to work to provide funds for its homeland. In 1966 Bhutan, claiming the Snowman as its "national animal," issued a set of commemorative stamps with various versions of the beast.

and this most popular of mysteries may become a mystery no more."

Why has our imagination been so captured by the Yeti? It cannot just have been the kind of news coverage it got. Publicity could have been responsible for a Seven Days' Wonder, but not for the fact that in the 25 years since the publication of Eric Shipton's photographs, the yeti has become firmly established in people's minds—almost part of folk history. It may be that we have a desire to discover lost peoples or creatures akin to humans. But, although the discovery of unknown tribes of about 100,000 people in New Guinea in 1954 created interest, it did not capture public imagination in the same way as the Yeti. The people of New Guinea are now a fact. The Yeti is still a mystery. We do

Left and below: three creatures, each of which has been proposed by experts as the real Abominable Snowman. At the far left is a composite drawing of a Yeti, as witnesses report it to appear; in the center is a red bear which Charles Stonor, formerly with the London Zoo, suggested might fit at least some of the Yeti descriptions; and below, a langur monkey, which the British Museum in 1937 felt was the only rational explanation for the footprints.

not know whether it exists or not. The only evidence we have is footprints and occasional sightings—not enough to form a scientific theory, but enough to stimulate our curiosity.

Perhaps this is the function that the Yeti serves for most of us. We need creatures to inhabit that strange borderland between fact and fantasy, and our interest lies not so much in whether they really exist, but in the possibility that they may exist. It is as if the very uncertainty, the remoteness, and the scanty evidence on which our ideas are based, increases the hold on us, and gives life an extra dimension it would lose if final proof came. These large creatures hovering between man and ape, grappling with nature to survive, satisfy a psychological need for many of us—just as dragons and mermaids did for our ancestors.

7

North American Monsters

North America has its own equivalent of the Yeti, which is known as the Bigfoot in the United States and the Sasquatch in Canada. Like the Yeti, these creatures are said to be hairy, to walk on two feet, and to resemble humans in appearance. For centuries the American Indians had passed on stories of the Bigfoot, whose footprints were said to measure anything from 16 to 22 inches, and whose height when fully grown was thought to be from 7 to 12 feet. The creature also featured in the folklore of South and Central America. This fact is emphasized by Dr. John Napier, curator of the primate collection of the Smithsonian Institution, who

Out of the dense California forest looms the giant figure of a man— but is it real? This one is not. It is an eight-foot redwood statue of a Bigfoot, North America's own equivalent to Asia's Abominable Snowman. Stories of the Bigfoot— called Sasquatch in Canada—are old and many, and as difficult of proof as the reports of the Yeti. This wooden figure was done by Jim McClarin, and is an attraction of the town of Willow Creek.

"Wild men of the woods..."

Above: an artist's conception of a Sasquatch, whose name comes from an Indian word that means "hairy giant." The Sasquatch is said to be up to 12 feet tall. Below: the "S-map" suggested by Snowman enthusiast Odette Tchernine as a theory of the distribution of the Snowman and its apparently closely related North American friends, the equally mysterious and elusive Bigfoot and Sasquatch monsters.

writes in his book *Bigfoot*, published in 1973: "Although in the last 20 years there has been a tremendous revival of public interest since these creatures have come to the attention of the 'white settlers,' it is a reasonable assumption, from what we know of early written records that, like Peyton Place, the story of Sasquatch has been continuing for a great many years."

The first recorded sighting of a Sasquatch track by a non-Indian occurred in what is now Jasper, Alberta, in 1811. While crossing the Rockies in an attempt to reach the Columbia River, the explorer and trader David Thompson came across a set of strange footprints measuring 14 inches long by 8 inches wide. Four toe marks were shown in the deep snow. This was unlike the five-toe print of a bear, and convinced those who heard of the track that it did not belong to a grizzly. About 70 years after this, on July 4, 1884, an account of the capture of a supposed Sasquatch appeared in the *Daily Colonist*, the leading paper of British Columbia. The creature—subsequently nicknamed Jacko—had been spotted by the crew of a train traveling along the Fraser River between the towns of Lytton and Yale. The railmen had stopped the train, given chase to the gorilla-like being with coarse, black hair, and, on catching it, had placed it safely in the guard's van. After being on show for the citizens of Yale and the surrounding country for a time, Jacko was sold to Barnum and Bailey's Circus.

As time went on and more and more giant "wild men of the woods" were seen and written about, it became clear to experts that these creatures were more violent and dangerous than their kin the Yeti. This was confirmed in 1910 when two prospectors, brothers named MacLeod, were found in the Nahanni Valley in the Northwest Territories of Canada with their heads cut off. The Sasquatches who had been seen in the area were blamed for the double murder, and from then on the area became known as Headless Valley. Eight years later the fearful

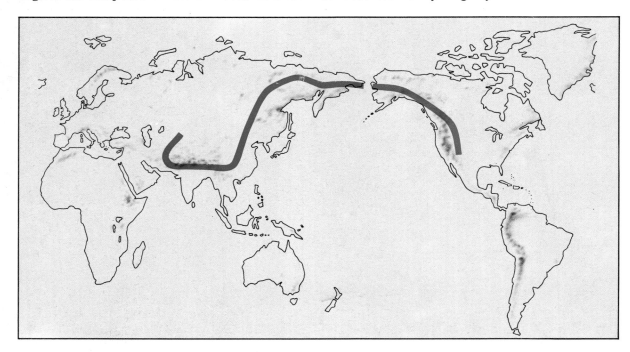

Bigfoot struck again with an attack on a prospector's shack in Mount St. Lawrence, Washington. According to the *Seattle Times*, which reported the incident, the assailants were about eight feet tall, were "half-human, half-monster," and were able to hypnotize people, to use ventriloquism, and to make themselves invisible at will.

Throughout the next few decades the Sasquatch and Bigfoot made frequent and much-publicized appearances in British Columbia, Northern California, and the state of Washington. One of the most fully documented accounts took place in 1924 in British Columbia.

At first, the few people who heard it refused to believe lumberjack Albert Ostman's story of being kidnapped in the mountainous hinterland of British Columbia, of being kept prisoner in a remote "cliff-enclosed" valley for more than a week, and of escaping from his "relentless captors" and making his way thankfully back to civilization. What caused his friends and family to doubt his tale was the fact that his kidnappers, so he said, were no ordinary hoodlums or gangsters. They were a family—father, mother, teenage son, and young daughter— but a family of "near-human hairy beasts." According to Ostman, he fell into their clutches in the summer of 1924 while on vacation. Having decided to mix business with pleasure, he had traveled to the head of Toba Inlet, near Vancouver Island, to look for traces of the gold that had formerly been mined there. Equipped with a rifle, cooking utensils, and cans of food, he spent some six or seven days roaming through the district. He got farther and farther off the beaten track. Finally he came across a secluded glade surrounded by cypress trees and containing a tempting freshwater spring in its center. Tired but contented, he resolved to spend some time there, and pitched his sleeping bag beneath the stars. On the second night in the glade, however, he woke up to find himself being carried "inside my bag like a sack of potatoes, the only thing in sight being a huge hand clutching the partly closed neck of the bag."

Ostman's kidnapper walked rapidly, and the journey was rough and painful for the bagged lumberjack. He was glad when the bag was suddenly dropped on the ground and he was able to crawl out of it. Dazed and bruised he looked around him, and met the curious stares of a weird family—all huge, hairy, and beastlike. Ostman feared for his life, but his giant captors did not bother him. In fact, they even allowed him to prepare his own meals from his supply of canned provisions. They turned out to be vegetarians who ate sweet grass, roots, and spruce tips from the evergreen forests. They also gave him a certain amount of freedom to explore his new valley home. Ostman noticed that it was the mother and son who did the family chores, wandering off into the trees and returning with tubers and hemlock tips. The father and daughter kept a careful watch over him.

Ostman feared he might be meant for the daughter later. It was this consideration, plus the obvious fact that he did not want to spend the rest of his life as the family's pet, that made Ostman resolve to escape. He got away one day when his kidnappers had become so used to him that they seemed to

Kidnapped by the Hairy Monsters

Albert Ostman, a Canadian lumberjack, in 1924 combined a vacation with a bit of gold prospecting. He camped near the head of the Toba Inlet opposite Vancouver Island, spent a week exploring, and decided to stop in a lovely glade under some cypress trees. The second night there he awoke to find himself being carried away in his sleeping bag like a sack of potatoes. He saw a huge hand around the partly open neck of the bag.

When Ostman was later dumped out on the ground, he was in the middle of a family of four big-footed monsters—the Sasquatch or Bigfeet. They were all enormous and hairy: father, who had kidnapped him, mother, a nearly adult son, and a younger daughter. The father was eight feet tall, the mother about seven. For six days Ostman was held prisoner, though no harm was done him. He observed that they were vegetarians, eating the grass, roots, and spruce tips gathered mainly by the mother and son. The daughter and father kept an eye on Ostman, but grew increasingly trustful of him. Finally he got the chance to escape.

Fearing to be locked away as a madman, Ostman said nothing publicly about his adventure for many years.

Above: John Green, author and intrepid investigator of Bigfoot stories. Here he is studying a set of 15-inch footprints found on Blue Creek Mountain in northern California in 1967.

think he was as happy in the wilds as they were, and so let their vigilance slip temporarily. On his return home Ostman was at first reluctant to tell of his unique and unsettling experience. Those whom he did mention it to regarded him as a crank—or worse. So he said no more about it until 33 years later in 1957. Only then did he come forward and tell newspapermen and anthropologists of his enforced stay with the monstrous family. Asked why he hadn't made a public statement earlier, he understandably replied that he had thought no one would take him seriously—or even that they might question his state of mind. In a belated attempt to gain credence, he swore the truth of his story before a Justice of the Peace at Fort Langley, British Columbia, on August 20, 1957, and later agreed to be interviewed by experts.

Ostman's account appeared honest in most respects, but his report of the creatures' eating habits did cause doubt. Considering that the Sasquatch family in all must have weighed more than 2000 pounds—as much as five male gorillas or fourteen adult humans, for example, it seemed unlikely that such outsize beings could have kept alive and active on the kind of low-calorie diet Ostman described. The province's Minister for Recreation and Conservation received a report from Frank L. Beebe of the British Columbia Provincial Museum in 1967. In it the expert stated that the type of vegetation used by Ostman's giants "produces the very poorest quality of low-energy food and the least quantity of high-energy food of any forest type on the planet."

A look back at the year that Ostman actually claimed to have met up with the Sasquatches revealed that 1924 had also provided another version of the monsters' activities. This time the incident took place in Ape Canyon, Washington. It was there that a group of coal miners were attacked by a "horde of Bigfeet" after one of the workers, Fred Beck, had met a Bigfoot at the edge of a canyon, and, terrified, had shot it three times in the back. A running battle then ensued between the dead monster's companions and the miners. It ended with the Bigfeet driving the panic stricken men from the area forever. Beck's version, as told to two well-known Bigfoot investigators, was given by Dr. John Napier in his book *Bigfoot*:

"At night the apes counterattacked, opening the assault by knocking a heavy strip of wood out from between two logs of the miners' cabin. After that there were assorted poundings on the walls, door, and roof, but the building was designed to withstand heavy mountain snows and the apes failed to break in . . . There was . . . the sound of rocks hitting the roof and rolling off, and [the miners] did brace the heavy door from the inside. They heard creatures thumping around on top of the cabin as well as battering the walls, and they fired shots through the walls and roof without driving them away. The noise went on from shortly after dark until nearly dawn . . . The cabin had no windows and of course no one opened the door, so in fact the men inside did not see what was causing the commotion outside. Nor could Mr. Beck say for sure . . . that there were more than two creatures outside. There were that many because there had been one on the roof and one pounding the wall

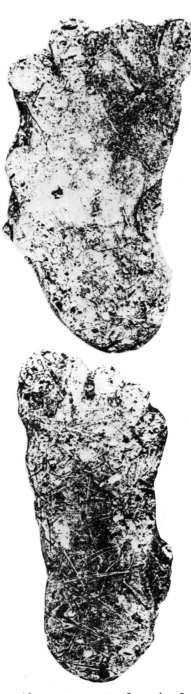

Above: two casts of a pair of
human-type footprints of great
size even for a Bigfoot—they
measure 17½ inches long. The
left foot (top) is deformed: the
unfortunate Bigfoot appears
to have a clubfoot, probably
from an injury during its youth.

Right: Green with a footprint cast
he presented to a local museum.
Officials declared it to be a fake.

123

simultaneously. However many there were, it was enough for the miners, who packed up and abandoned their mine the next day."

In 1940 a Bigfoot male that was eight-foot tall raided a farmstead in Nevada. The farmer's wife had to grab her children and flee. When she came back later, she found the house encircled by huge footprints. A large barrel of salted fish had also been knocked over and its contents spilled. In 1958 a truck driver named Jerry Crew found some impressively big tracks in the California mud. He followed them up hill and down into low ground before sensibly taking a plaster cast of one of them. He had himself photographed holding the cast up, and the picture caused a sensation in the newspapers and periodicals in which it appeared. Five years later Texas oil millionaire Tom Slick died in a crash in his private plane while trying to get at the truth about the Bigfoot. The findings of the various expeditions he financed have never been made public. However, the stories about his Bigfoot searches kept the interest in the monster alive. Between June 1964 and December 1970, 25 Bigfoot sightings were reported, bringing the grand total of eye-witness reports of footprints and monsters to more than 300. In 1969 in Canada alone there were no less than 60 different accounts of Sasquatches and their doings.

Toward the end of the 1960s came a publicity stunt involving the Bigfoot. It was known that the monsters were usually seen in midsummer or fall. Operating on this knowledge, a one-time rodeo worker, Roger Patterson, announced in October 1967 that he and a half-Indian friend had encountered a female Bigfoot near Bluff Creek, California, and had taken 20 feet of film of her as she ambled along the outskirts of a dense forest. Patterson said he operated the camera while on the run, and that explained why the opening frames of his 16mm color movie jumped about so much. The film was of a creature some seven feet high and weighing between 350 and 450 pounds. It was shown to Dr. Napier, who duly noted its heavy build, reddish-brown hair, and prominent furry breasts and buttocks.

Dr. Napier viewed the movie six times at a private screening in Washington, D.C. on December 2, 1967, before forming an opinion about it. He was dissatisfied with the alleged Bigfoot's "self-conscious walk," which seemed to him to be that of a human male. He felt that the cone-shaped top of the skull was "definitely nonhuman," but was suspicious of the being's center of gravity—as he said, "precisely as it is in modern man"—and could only accept the buttocks as a "human hallmark."

"The upper half of the body," he went on, "bears some resemblence to an ape, and the lower half is typically human. It is almost impossible to conceive that such structural hybrids could exist in nature. One half of the animal must be artificial. In view of the walk, it can only be the upper half. Subsequently, I have seen and studied the film, frame by frame, a dozen times or more . . . I was [also] puzzled by the extraordinary exaggeration of the walk: it seemed to me to be an overstatement of the normal pattern, a bad actor's interpretation of a classical human walking gait . . . There is little doubt that the scientific evidence taken collectively points to a hoax of some kind. The creature

Below: Rene Dahinden (on left) the Swiss-Canadian investigator into the Sasquatch, with Roger Patterson, who claimed to have taken approximately 100 feet of color movie film of a female Bigfoot wandering through a California forest in 1967. They are holding plaster casts of footprints of manlike animals that they identify as Bigfeet.

Above and right: a frame from the movie Patterson shot, with an enlargement of the creature herself. She has a cone-shaped skull, which is a characteristic of large adult male gorillas and orang-utans, and she also seems to have furry but otherwise human buttocks and breasts. Her walk was described by experts as that of a self-conscious human.

shown in the film does not stand up well to functional analysis. There are too many inconsistencies . . . Perhaps it was a man dressed up in a monkey-skin; if so it was a brilliantly executed hoax and the unknown perpetrator will take his place with the great hoaxers of the world." By the time Dr. Napier had reached this last conclusion, the film had been shown commercially to audiences both in Canada and the United States.

A couple of years after the Patterson film, a sensational headline in the *National Bulletin* screamed, "I Was Raped by the Abominable Snowman." The rape victim, a young woman by the name of Helen Westring, claimed that she had met her assailant some three years earlier while on a solo hunting trip in the woods near Bemidji, Minnesota. Hypnotizing her with its pink eyes, she said, the monster with huge hairy hands and long arms had ripped her clothes off "like one would peel a banana." It then stared at her intently, particularly at "the area between my legs," threw her to the ground, and went about its "beastly purpose." Fortunately for the victim she fainted; on coming to she took her rifle and shot the rapist through the right eye.

As the story unfolded it was clear that Helen Westring was not talking about a Bigfoot, and that the newspaper was capitalizing on the wide interest in the Himalayan Abominable Snowman by using such a headline. The gory rape-murder story referred instead to the Minnesota Iceman, who was famous in

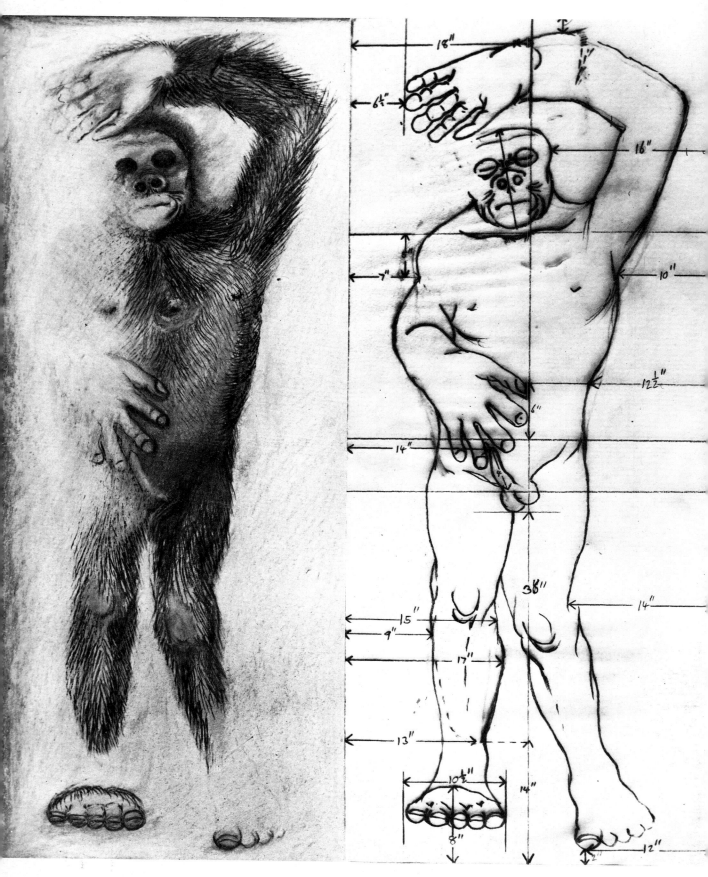

his own right as a monster—and, possibly, as the biggest hoax of the century.

In the late 1960s, the Minnesota Iceman was taken around the carnivals and fairgrounds of the United States, and shown to vast audiences for 25 cents admission. The "mysterious hairy body" was in the possession of Frank Hansen who, in May 1967, first exhibited the so-called "man left over from the ice age" to the American public. Hansen claimed that the body on display had been found preserved in a 6000-pound block of ice in the Bering Straits.

For more than 18 months the monster was taken from area to area. News of its existence spread until it was heard by the well-known Belgian scientist and writer Dr. Bernard Heuvelmans and his associate Ivan Sanderson. The two men journeyed to inspect the Iceman at Hansen's farm near Winona, Minnesota out of their interest in monsters, for by then the creature's identification as a prehistoric man had seemed to evaporate. They found him encased in a block of ice and enclosed in a refrigerated coffin. The monster's right eye had been penetrated by a bullet and the back of his skull shattered. Hansen said he had been murdered. Their examination began on December 17, 1968, and, although it lasted for two days, they had only restricted access to the creature. The coffin was kept in a small poorly lit trailer, and in order to sketch the Iceman, Sanderson had to lie on top of the plate glass lid of the coffin, his nose almost touching that of the monster's. Photographs were also taken. Heuvelmans later wrote a paper for the Royal Institute of Natural Sciences in Belgium, which he called "Preliminary Note on a Specimen preserved in ice; an unknown living hominid." From this it seemed that the two scientists had accepted the Iceman as fact, and Hansen's explantion as to the bullet wound on the monster as truth. Heuvelmans statement was given by Odette Tchernine in her book *The Yeti* as:

"The speciman at first sight is representative of man . . . of fairly normal proportions, but excessively hairy . . . His skin is of the waxlike color characteristic of corpses of men of white race when not tanned by the sun . . . The damage to the occiput [back of the head], and the fact that the eyeballs had been ejected from their sockets, one having completely disappeared, suggests that the creature had been shot in the face by several large-caliber bullets. One bullet must have penetrated the cubitus [forearm] when he tried to protect himself. A second bullet pierced the right eye, destroying it, and causing the other to start out of its cavity. This caused the much larger cavity at the back of the cranium, producing immediate death."

With the Iceman's acceptance both in popular and academic circles, Hansen then announced that the creature, nicknamed "Bozo" by Sanderson, was not his at all: he was merely its keeper. Its real owner was a mysterious "Mr X," a millionaire Hollywood film maker who had bought the Iceman from an emporium in Hong Kong, and had had it flown to the United States. If Hansen was to be believed, Bozo had been shuttled around the Far East from Soviet sealers, to Japanese whalers, to Chinese dealers, all the while causing consternation of Customs and other officials. The Hollywood tycoon was said to be interested only in allowing ordinary people to view their "Neanderthal ancestor," and so in 1969 the Iceman returned to the carnival circuits. This time he was billed as a "Creature frozen and preserved forever in a coffin of ice" in a return to the prehistoric man idea. It was apparent to those who saw it that the second exhibit was no fossil.

As it happened, Sanderson had approached Dr. John Napier just before the carnival tour to see if he might be interested in having the monster fully and scientifically investigated. At first Napier was enthusiastic to undertake a study. But then a number of things happened to squash his enthusiasm. First, the Secretary of the Smithsonian, S. Dillon Ripley, learned from Hansen that the creature about to go on exhibition was a latex model, which, Hansen was careful to say, resembled the original Iceman. Second, after the murder theory was put forward, Ripley immediately wrote to the FBI to see if the Bureau would cooperate in tracing the original exhibit. As no federal law had been broken, the Bureau would not intervene—but this did not stop Hansen from preparing a new display sign for his monster, calling it "The near-Man . . . Investigated by the FBI."

The Smithsonian then withdrew its interest in the Iceman, which only seemed to spur Hanson on. He held a press conference at his ranch, timing it prior to taking the Iceman to St. Paul. He admitted to reporter Gorden Yeager of the *Rochester Post-Bulletin* that the monster was "man-made, an illusion." From St. Paul the exhibit moved to Grand Rapids where it was filmed by a team from *Time-Life*. This film showed distinct differences between the model then on display and the Iceman as drawn and photographed by Heuvelmans and Sanderson. The original creature had only one yellowish tooth, while this one boasted at least four.

After the Helen Westring story of the murder of the Minnesota Iceman, Hansen came up with a final version of how the monster had met his death. In *Saga* magazine in 1970 he declared that it was he, not Helen Westring, who had shot the monster in the woods. He had done so while in the US Air Force on a hunting trip with some fellow officers in the north of the state. The creature had fallen mortally wounded in the snow, and had stayed there for two months until Hansen removed the body to the deep-freeze at his camp quarters. "Let's not tell a single person about this," he warned his wife. "We'll just leave it there until Spring." After seven years, Hansen took the corpse to his nearby farm. Later, and for reasons never explained, he had a latex replica made of it by special technicians in Hollywood. From then on he simply switched the exhibits when necessary, and talked as fast as he could in order to fool the press, the public, and the experts.

One person who didn't believe Hansen's "transparently dubious" confession is Dr. Napier, who is as close to the story as anyone. But however skeptical he is about the Iceman, he feels that the "North American Bigfoot or Sasquatch has a lot going for it . . . Too many people claim to have seen it, or at least to have seen footprints, to dismiss its reality out of hand. To suggest that hundreds of people at worst are lying or, at best, deluding themselves is neither proper nor realistic."

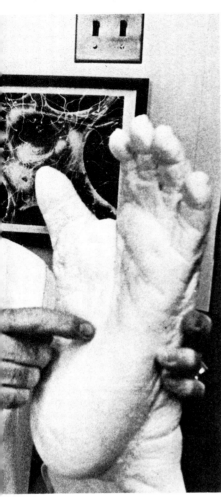

Above: Dr. Joeffrey H. Bourne of the Yerkes Regional Primate Center in Georgia, holding a print of a gorilla's foot. Like many scientists, he believes the existence of giant humanoids such as the Yeti and the Bigfoot is possible, but decidedly unproved.

Left: Henry McDaniel, a disabled war veteran of Illinois, showing the size of footprints he said were made by a gray, hairy, three-legged monster with pink eyes bulging from a huge head. He claims he saw the thing twice.

Right: another alleged Bigfoot photo, taken somewhere northeast of Spokane, Washington. Skeptics remark on the odd similarity of the Bigfoot's method of descent with that of a cowardly human.

8

The Monster Business

We have always been of two minds about our monsters. Although in a sense we have tried to conquer them, we have also in a sense yielded to them. Monsters of old usually inhabited some difficult and inaccessible place. For many people today the scientific laboratory is difficult and inaccessible—as frightening as the dragon's cave was to our ancestors. Monsters, usually developed under extraordinary circumstances, have extraordinary features and can only be destroyed by special skills and equipment. Perseus needed winged sandals, a helmet of invisibility, and a mirror to kill the Gorgon. If he had looked at the horrible creature he would have turned to

Are there real monsters hidden in the distant and inaccessible parts of the world? We play with the question, and while waiting for the answer, keep ourselves happily frightened with fictional creations guaranteed to make us shiver with dread, and settle into our movie seats with anticipation. Right: Boris Karloff, best-known of the actors who have portrayed Frankenstein's man-made monster, in the *Bride of Frankenstein*. It was filmed in Hollywood in 1935.

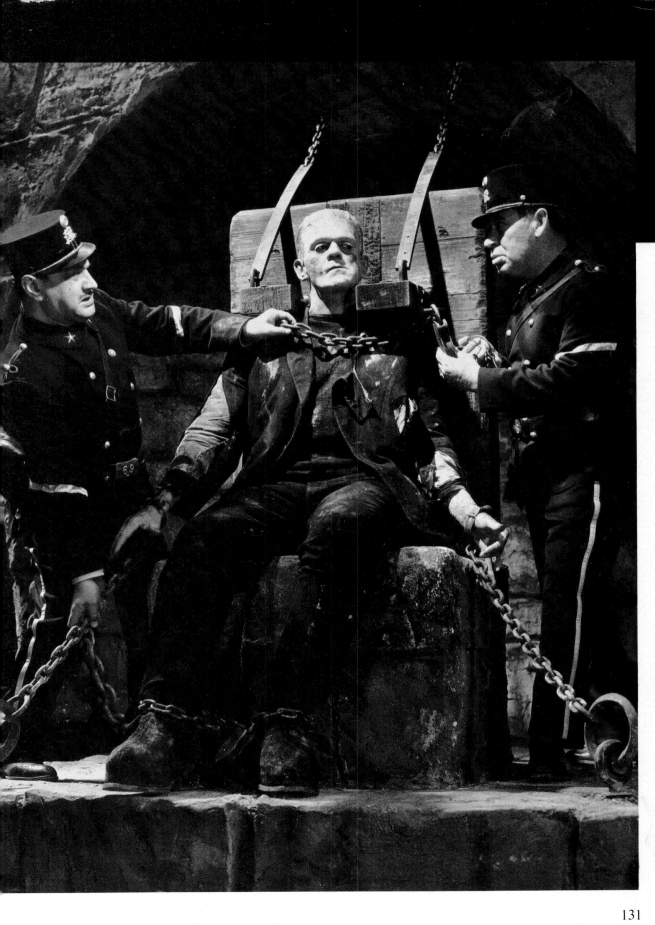

"I saw the hideous phantasm of a man stretched out..."

Above: Mary Wollstonecraft Shelley, the wife of the poet and the sweet-faced creator of the classic horror tale *Frankenstein*.

stone. St. George needed Christian faith and courage to master the dragon. In our time, a scientific formula is usually more appropriate.

As our understanding of our own emotional responses increased, some people became aware of the possibility of creating fictional monsters for commercial ends. Just the right mixture of terror and sex could provide safe and pleasureable titillation for the public—and profit for the creators.

The monster business might be said to have started more than 150 years ago when a young English girl went to Switzerland for vacation. The girl, 21-year-old Mary Wollstonecraft Shelley, had run away to the continent four years earlier with poet Percy Bysshe Shelley. They had lived together without marriage until the death of his wife allowed their marriage to take place in 1816. Two years later, in the wet and miserable Swiss summer of 1818, they were staying with their friend, the poet Lord Byron, on the shores of Lake Geneva. For entertainment at night Byron, the Shelleys, and a doctor friend sat around a blazing log fire reading volumes of German ghost stories. After enduring several days of cold and constant rain, Byron suggested that each of the four of them should write a "truly horrific" story for amusement. The winner of the literary contest would be the person who succeeded in scaring the others most.

By the term ghost story, Byron said he meant anything that depicted the "monstrous, the horrendous, the unusual." Mary Shelley, who had never written anything before, naturally experienced the greatest creative difficulty. "I busied myself to think of a story—a story to rival those which had excited us to this task," she stated. "One which would speak to the mysterious fears of our nature and awaken thrilling horror—one to make the reader dread to look around, to curdle the blood, and quicken the beatings of the heart. If I did not accomplish these things, my ghost story would be unworthy of its name."

Morning after morning she confessed to her competitors that inspiration had not come in the night. Evening after evening she listened to the long and macabre conversations between the two major poets. Their talk centered mostly around the experiments being made at the time by an English doctor who, it was said, could make a "piece of vermicelli in a glass case" move "by some extraordinary means . . . with voluntary motion." This led them to such statements as: "Perhaps a corpse could be reanimated; perhaps the component parts of a creature might be manufactured, brought together, and [given] vital warmth." It was after midnight when this particular discussion ended, and Mary Shelley and her husband went wearily to bed. However, tired as she was, she had difficulty sleeping. Later she wrote of the extraordinary vision that came to her in a kind of waking dream.

"I saw—with shut eyes, but acute mental vision—I saw the pale student of unhallowed arts kneeling beside the thing he had put together. I saw the hideous phantasm of a man stretched out, and then, on the working of some powerful engine, show signs of life and stir with an uneasy, half-vital motion. Frightful it must be, for supremely frightful would be the effect of any human endeavor to mock the stupendous mechanism of the Creator of the world."

FRANKENSTEIN,

BY

MARY W. SHELLEY.

The day of my departure at length arrived.

LONDON:
COLBURN AND BENTLEY
NEW BURLINGTON, STREET.
1831.

Above: the title page of Mary Shelley's *Frankenstein*, which was published in London in 1831. Below: the popularity of the novel naturally led to a stage version. This engraving of 1850 shows a scene from the production entitled *Frankenstein, or, The Model Man*, as it was presented at the Adelphi Theater in London.

Below: an engraving from the 1831 edition of *Frankenstein*. The gloomy scene with the monster stirring captures the frightful moment when "by the glimmer of the half-extinguished light I saw the dull, yellow eye of the creature open; it breathed hard and a convulsive motion agitated its limbs . . . I rushed out of the room."

Above: publicity for the movie
Frankenstein—here, a poster for
display outside the theater—
made the sexual aspect explicit.

Below: this scene of the monster
and a little girl was too strong
for 1931, and was cut. In it, the
monster encounters a small girl
floating flowers in the river,
and happily joins in. When they
run out of flowers, he unthinkingly
throws her in. She doesn't float.

"He [the student] would hope that, left to itself, the slight
spark of life which he had communicated would fade, that this
thing which had received such imperfect animation would sub-
side into dead matter, and he might sleep in the belief that the
silence of the grave would quench forever the transient existence
of the hideous corpse which he had looked upon as the cradle of
life. He sleeps; but he is awakened; he opens his eyes; behold,
the horrid thing stands at his bedside, opening his curtains and
looking on him with yellow, watery, but speculative eyes. I opened
mine in terror."

That night, Baron Victor Frankenstein and the monster he
made in his laboratory were born. From then on the inhabitants
—especially the young girls—of the fictitious village of Ingold-
stad, Transylvania, would sleep uneasily in their beds. A monster
was in their midst, and there was no more peace. Little realizing
that she had created a classic theme of sexual potency and fear,
Mary Shelley gleefully reported the next morning that she had
thought of "a few pages, of a short tale." Shelley was so intrigued by her idea that he urged her to develop it at greater
length. So she wrote more, produced the novel called *Frankenstein, Or, The Modern Prometheus*, and bid her "hideous
progeny" to "go forth and prosper." The book did exactly that,
making her reputation and starting her on a writing career.

Over the years the book went into edition after edition, but in
1931 it reached an even wider audience when Hollywood filmed
it as *Frankenstein* with the then unknown Boris Karloff as the
man-made monster. By then the novel's sexual implications were
seen and better understood: the monster, though only half a
human, had the drives of a man and wanted a mate like other men.
Of course, Hollywood was wary of making the sexual content too
explicit, and the director compromised by limiting the monster's
attempts to take a mate to one time. He approaches a child whom
he discovers floating petals in a lake, and although his advances
are innocuous enough, he ends up by killing the youngster and
throwing her into the water. This scene was considered too
brutal for the sensibilities of the time, and it was cut before the
film was released. But in the sequel, *Bride of Frankenstein*, made
four years later, the monster's sex life was openly admitted. It
was handled by the creation of a wife, played by Elsa Lanchester.
"With Karloff," writes film historian Carlos Clarens in his book
Horror Movies, "she manages to communicate . . . a delicate
suggestion of the both the wedding bed and the grave."

By the early 20th century it had become obvious that most
monster stories—and the films inspired by them—were little
more than sex sagas in disguise. In the 20th century it was no
longer enough to fob readers and audiences off with what the
Scottish prayer calls ". . . ghoulies and ghosties and long-leggety
beasties/And things that go bump in the night. . . ." There had to
be spicier nocturnal goings on, activities that appealed to the
beast in people and to primitive instincts. "Rather than sheer
perversity," Clarens asserts, "horror films require of the audience
a certain sophistication, a recognition of their mythical core, a
fascination of the psyche."

This angle had been appreciated before Hollywood brought
sex into its monster pictures. It was one of the most exploited

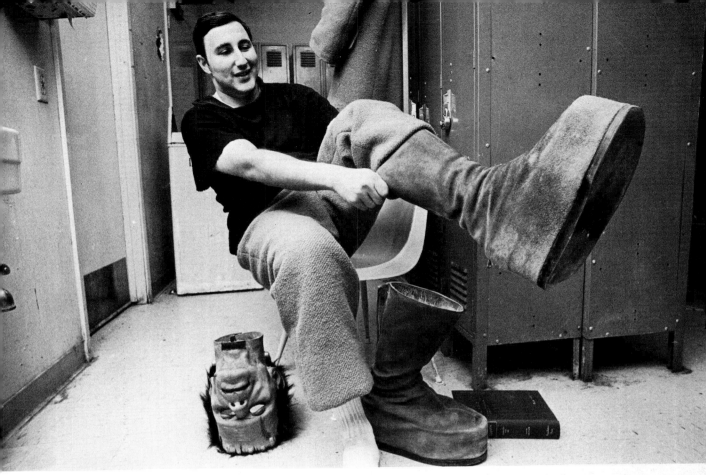

factors in early German films. The basic theme was that of the fairy tale's Beauty and the Beast, of the beautiful and virginal princess forced to live with a monster that both repels and fascinates her. In the fairy story the princess' love frees the beast from an evil spell, and turns him into a handsome prince who marries her. However, things did not always work out as happily in celluloid life. In *The Golem*, made in Berlin in 1914, a giant clay statue is bought by an antiquarian and brought to life by magic. The Golem becomes the antiquarian's servant, but falls in love with his master's young and desirable daughter. Sickened by the monster's attentions and appearance, she spurns him. The Golem goes berserk. After creating havoc, he falls to his death from a tower, an obvious phallic symbol, and the girl's purity is preserved.

Monsters became bolder as time went on. They were no longer content to gaze down upon their adored one as she slept. They picked her up bodily and carried her away over marshes, across swamps, into jungles, and up alleyways. The heroines were always in danger of being ravished by the beasts, but the implication was that they might have dreamed about or secretly and subconsciously yearned for this fate. The idea of sleep—the unreal events within it and the realities without—was expanded in the 1919 classic *The Cabinet of Dr. Caligari*. This film, which deals with a man who seduces and kills women while he is hypnotized, was based on a real-life sex murder in which a human monster raped and murdered a girl at a fair in Hamburg. The film monster is a staring sleep walker who snatches a nubile

Above: the Frankenstein monster became part of the entertainment on Universal Studio tours. Here a guide gets into monster gear. Below: in his gruesome costume, which the tourists seem to love, the guide greets excited visitors at the starting point of their trip around the famous studio.

brunette from her bed and flees with her over rooftops and fields. He is pursued by the townsfolk, and dies of exhaustion. Once again the maiden survives, and we know she will find a lover who is well-intentioned and acceptable.

The females in *The Head of Janus*, made in 1920, were less fortunate. For the first time on the screen monsters influenced the behavior of the mildest and most respectable of men. The upstanding hero, played by Conrad Veidt, has an obsession for the two-faced Roman god Janus, representing the good and the evil in man. Influenced by the evil side, Veidt becomes a vicious sex criminal. First he assaults his fiancée and forces her to work in a brothel, and then he attacks and kills a small girl in the street. In the end he dies by swallowing poison. Audiences have learned to their horror that wickedness and lust are contagious, and it is not enough merely to defy monsters. Each of us must also beware that we do not start to behave like a monster, assaulting and degrading those nearest and dearest to us.

It was not until 1925 that the concept of beauty and the beast

Above: Lon Chaney, the man of a thousand disguises (most of them usually repellent), became *The Phantom of the Opera*, made in 1925. This scene is of the ghastly moment when the girl, played by Mary Philbin, snatches off the phantom's ever-present mask and sees his visage in all its horror.

was presented both with realism and chilling fantasy. The film was *The Phantom of the Opera* in the first of three versions made by Hollywood. The star was Lon Chaney. The scene is Paris where a hideously disfigured creature lurks in the catacomb of cellars beneath the Opera House. Despite his handicaps he is madly in love with a young soprano, and does all he can to aid her career. Her success pleases him, but he is not satisfied until he has lured her down to his dank and watery living quarters. There he keeps her captive in a weird and gruesome bridal suite. Reaching a dramatic climax in the movie, the heroine tears the mask from her captor's face, and recoils in horror and disgust at the sight of his disfigurement. The film ends with a mob invading the phantom's subterranean chambers and killing him. Some commentators have seen the film as deeper and more symbolic than just another shocker. The mask the phantom wears, they say, is that of every man who devotedly and courteously woos the girl of his choice. Behind this mask of conventionality, however, is the real person: a leering, unscrupulous

Above: a chilling scene of murder from *The Mummy's Ghost*, made in 1944. In this gruesome fancy, Lon Chaney plays the mummy that returns to life after being buried for thousands of years. He tries to kidnap the beatiful young girl who is the reincarnation of his ancient love—and goes on a murderous spree in the process.

Above: the huge gorilla in *The Murders in the Rue Morgue* bearing yet another luscious lady off to his psychopathic master, a doctor who is carrying out secret grotesque experiments. Bela Lugosi, who was best known as Dracula, played the doctor in this 1931 Hollywood movie.

sex fiend who thinks of nothing of subjecting his chosen one to imprisonment, bondage, and rape.

With the phantom setting box office records—and making people realize that there was probably a Frankenstein's monster hidden somewhere in all of us—American film makers turned from human to animal monsters. The increasing number of reports that giant creatures existed in remote parts of the world sent producers to stories such as Edgar Allan Poe's *Murders in the Rue Morgue*. Again Paris is the setting, again a lustful monster is on the loose. In the movie version, which differs from the original work, the monster is a huge gorilla employed by a mad doctor to kidnap women for his "unholy experiments." The gorilla carries out his task with relish. There are gruesome scenes of a prostitute bleeding to death on a torture rack, and of a dead woman shoved into a chimney upside down. Once more the monster carries the scantily dressed heroine over rooftops in the dark of night, and once more the women in the audience shivered—as much with pleasurable anticipation as with fear, some analysts would say.

As aware as any psychiatrist of the underlying sexual content in such plots—and of the second-hand thrills that they provided—the movie moguls looked for the ultimate in monster-and-sex stories. One producer felt he had found it in *King Kong*, which had been partly written by the English thriller writer Edgar Wallace.

Above: Hollywood hadn't invented horror. Back in the 1870s the Illustrated Police News thrilled London readers with real-life sensational blood and gore. (If real-life proved a bit too tepid, it was embellished as necessary.) Here two women are overcome as the magazine headline screams "Murderous Attack by a Gorilla." Below: the gorilla charges on in *Gorilla at Large*, made in 1954.

It was released in 1933, and the producer was right: *King Kong* was a smash hit. In it the giant ape called King Kong snatched up the fair-haired heroine in one huge hand and made off with her into the wilderness. Puzzled by her strange, human, female smell, he at one point tears off her dress and sniffs the scent of her on his fingers. This was suggestiveness run riot, and Hollywood compensated for such blatancy by showing that the nice guy got the girl in the final reel—and that the beast in us was always rendered impotent. King Kong, like the Golem of 1914, dies in a tumble from what is clearly a phallic symbol—the Empire State Building, then the tallest in the world. The hero has the last word in the film, and it is a comment with sexual undertones. He says: "'Twas Beauty killed the Beast!" If the movie beast couldn't be transformed into an eligible prince charming then he had to die in order to observe the prevailing morality code. *King Kong*, which was a year in the making and had a huge budget for the period, was and still is the most famous of all monster movies.

There is at least one monster movie that was successful without the sex element. It was made in 1925 and was based on Sir Arthur Conan Doyle's novel *The Lost World*, published 13 years earlier. Conan Doyle had read a book on extinct animals by the zoology professor Ray Lankester, and was inspired by it. He was especially impressed by its illustrations of "nightmare-shapes of sabre-teeth and witless eyes," and thought it was not too fantastic that such creatures still existed. "Suppose," he said, "one misty evening, a stegosaurus came looming over the misty downs? Better still: suppose in some remote corner of the earth—a high plateau in the jungle, say, untouched and untouchable in primitive life—such creatures were yet alive? What game for a sportsman! What wonders for a zoologist!"

The repercussions to his book, which was a mixture of imaginitive fiction and solid fact, were immediate. Professor Lankester, author of the scientific work that had inspired Conan Doyle, wrote to him saying: "You are perfectly splendid in your story of the 'lost world' mountaintop. I feel proud to have had a certain small share in its inception ... I notice that you rightly withold any intelligence from the big dinosaurs, and also acute smell from the apemen." About a year after Conan Doyle's book appeared, a group of American explorers set out from Philadelphia in the yacht *Delaware* for the broad waters of the Amazon. According to a newspaper account of April 1, 1913: "The yacht is the property of the University of Pennsylvania, and is bound for Brazil with a daring party of explorers, who propose penetrating to the far reaches of the Amazon, and to the headwaters of many of its tributaries in the interest of science and humanity. They seek Conan Doyle's 'lost world,' or some scientific evidence of it." They were unsuccessful, but their very attempt demonstrated mankind's willingness—need, almost—to accept monsters as real.

It was not until the 1950s that there was a serious revival of the horror film, and it was then that such curiosities as the Yeti and the Loch Ness Monster came into their own. Movies ranging from *The Abominable Snowman of the Himalayas* to *The Monster That Challenged the World* were made about the Yeti or their kin. The trend continued into the 1960s, and today it is as strong if

Above: King Kong, carrying the hapless heroine in one huge hand, looms ominously over the tall skyscrapers of New York City.

not stronger than ever. We are living in what film director Alfred Hitchcock calls the Age of Monsters. "Monsters are all around us," he writes. "They abound on the motion picture screens, coming from the depths of the sea, from under the Arctic ice, from outer space, or other such unexplored regions." Recognizing that the desire to be shocked and shaken starts early, publishers are now putting out Make-Your-Own-Monster books which show children how to construct such long-lasting favorites as the bearded dragon, the dinosaur, the Golem, the lake monster, and the sea serpent. However, as Hitchcock points out, ". . . a monster does not have to be a beast so large he wipes out a suburb every time he lashes his tail. Nor does he have to be a roughly human-shaped creature with his head bolted to his neck."

There are also monsters of the soul, the mind, and the sub-conscious. It is apparent that men and women respond to mon-sters and mythic creatures, whether mermaids, unicorns, dragons or underwater snakes, in a way that is ambiguous and erotic. Monsters both stimulate and repel, excite and nauseate. On

King Kong created a perfect blend of monster-and-sex. The story was hardly a model of subtlety, but within it were opportunities to exploit every shiver of dread and gasp of astonished shock, and the movie used them skillfully. Audiences flocked in, and King Kong as the giant ape became a permanent addition to American folk imagination. Above: King Kong, straddling the Empire State Building, waves a plane around just before his fall.

Right: the giant ape torments some pursuers on his own home ground. He was hard to capture.

Right: the drawing of a monster that was used by Sir Arthur Conan Doyle to start the action in his popular 1912 novel *The Lost World*. In the book, this drawing is supposed to have been found in the sketchbook of a dead artist who had traveled in the Amazon. It was in hopes of proving the existence of such monsters that the fictional party of explorers sets off into the deep, unknown Amazonian jungle.

Below: the fictional Professor George E. Challenger, hero of *The Lost World*. This picture was used as the frontispiece in the 1912 edition of the novel.

Opposite: beyond the torrid and tangled Guyana jungle lie the sheer and unfriendly cliffs of the Roraima plateau—the real Lost World. This photograph was taken by an expedition in 1973. It took the team 17 days of inching along some of the world's most difficult terrain to reach the peak—and they could not stay to explore it. Couldn't Roraima—and places like it—be the home of monsters surviving from the past? What else could live there?

another and equally important level, our interest in monsters and mythic beasts seems to have much to do with an awe of hugeness, and an admiration of courage and fortitude in the face of forces of the unknown.

"On the one hand," anthropologist Dr. John Napier writes, "we are delighted when bigness is overthrown, be it the small and good overcoming the big and bad (David and Goliath) . . . or simply man putting a monster in its place (St. George and the dragon). It gives us great satisfaction to see financial barons topple, commercial empires dissolve, bosses dismissed, boxing champions knocked out, and the World Cup winners soundly beaten. On the other hand, man seems to admire the big instinctively: the tall man is often esteemed without regard to his capabilities, the tall building attracts our admiration, and the large animals . . . our benevolence. We both love and hate large size, depending on whether or not it constitutes a threat to our survival . . . I believe our attitude toward legendary monsters is equally ambivalent. We laugh at them and we fear them, we love them and we hate them, but overall in a curious way, we respect them simply for being monstrously big."

From primitive times to the present day human beings have needed monsters. Frightening though they may be, monsters nevertheless reduce to a comprehensible form our inner fears and dread of external forces beyond our control. Perhaps for the early Greek sailors a six-headed brute such as Scylla, who was said to suck men to their deaths under the sea, was a way of coming to terms with the arbitrary nature of the elements and the ever-present danger of drowning. In times when life for most people in many parts of the world was little more than a daily struggle for survival, dragons and other mythic beasts may have channeled people's anxieties away from disease, starvation, and invasion. More important, perhaps, fabulous creatures may have added an element of mystery and excitement to otherwise drab lives. With the progress of science and technology, we have unleashed a new set of fears to replace those we have conquered. Monsters are still with us. Today they spring from outer space or from the experimental laboratory.

Picture Credits

Key to picture positions: (T) top (C) center (B) bottom; and in combinations, e.g. (TR) top right (BL) bottom left

2 Kunstmuseum, Basel/Colorphoto Hans Hinz
4 Vatican Museum
6 Aldus Archives
7 National Gallery of Art Washington; Ailsa Mellon Bruce Fund
8(L) Alte Pinakothek, München/Photo Scala, Florence
9, 10 Giraudon
11(R) Reproduced by permission of the British Library Board
12(L) Condé, Chantilly/Giraudon
13 Giraudon
14 Ivan Polunin/Susan Griggs Agency
15(T) Gulbenkian Museum of Oriental Art, University of Durham/Photo Jeff Teasdale
16(T) Durham County Library
16(B) Aldus Archives
17 Mary Evans Picture Library
18(T) Aldus Archives
18(B) J.-L. Charmet, Paris
19 Mary Evans Picture Library
20(B) Snark International
21(T) Reproduced by permission of the British Library Board
21(B), 22(TL) Aldus Archives
22(TR) Mary Evans Picture Library
23 Bruce Coleman Ltd.
24 Snark International
25 Photo © J. G. Ferguson taken from The Raymond Mander and Joe Mitchenson Theatre Collection
26, 27 J.-L. Charmet, Paris
28(T) Aldus Archives
28(B) Museo degli Argenti, Firenze/Photo Scala
29 Michael Holford Library photo
30–2(T) Aldus Archives
32(B) R. Kinne/Photo Researchers, Inc.
34(T) Giraudon
35(T) Aldus Archives
35(B) Fotogram
36(L) Snark International
37-8 The Metropolitan Museum of Art, The Cloisters Collection, Gift of John D. Rockefeller, Jr., 1937
39 Giraudon
40(T) Aldus Archives
40(B) Photo Mike Busselle © Aldus Books
41(T) Bodleian Library, Oxford
41(B) Aldus Archives
43 J.-L. Charmet, Paris
44 Mary Evans Picture Library
45(L) Aldus Archives
45(R) Culver Pictures
46(T) Mary Evans Picture Library
46(B) Richard Orr/Linden Artists © Aldus Books
48-9 Gino d'Achille © Aldus Books
50(L) Aldus Archives

50(R) Michael Holford Library photo
51-3 Aldus Archives
54(T) Roger-Viollet
54(CL) Aldus Archives
54(CR) The Bettmann Archive
54(B) Courtesy of the New Brunswick Museum
56(T) Reproduced with the permission of the Naval Historical Foundation from a print owned by Rear Admiral Henry Williams
57(T) The Bettmann Archive
57(B), 58(T) Snark International
58(B) Compix, New York
59(C) Photo Penticton Herald
59(B) Central Press Photos
61(TL) Barnaby's Picture Library
61(TR) Popperfoto
61(BL) Stern Archiv
63 Keystone
64(L) Radio Times Hulton Picture Library
65(B) Photo Dmitri Kasterine © Aldus Books
66-7 Gino d'Achille © Aldus Books
68 London Daily Mail
69-71 Illustrated London News Press Association Ltd.
72(TL) Popperfoto
72(TR) Popperfoto
72(B) Keystone
74(T) Photo Tim Dinsdale
75(T) Aldus Archives
75(B) Compix, New York
76(T) The Associated Press Ltd.
76(B) Popperfoto
77 Compix, New York
78-81 Syndication International Ltd., London
82 The Associated Press Ltd.
83 London Express
85 Zdenek Burian, Life Before Man, by permission of the publishers, Artia, Prague
86 Culver Pictures
88-9 Gino d'Achille © Aldus Books
90(B) Aldus Archives
91(T) Zdenek Burian, Life Before Man, by permission of the publishers, Artia, Prague
91(B) Peabody Museum of Natural History, Yale University
92(T) Trustees of the British Museum (Natural History)
92(B) Bilderdienst Süddeutscher Verlag
93(T) London Daily Mail
93(B) Trustees of the British Museum (Natural History)
94 Zdenek Burian, Life Before Man, by permission of the publishers, Artia, Prague
95(T) Trustees of the British Museum Natural History)
95(B) Courtesy Pitman Publishing, London
96 Aldus Archives
98-9 Gino d'Achille © Aldus Books

100 Culver Pictures
101 Photo Don Whillans (Annapurna South Face Expedition, 1970)
102 Aldus Archives
103 Royal Geographical Society
104(B) London Daily Mail
105(T) Chris Bonington/Bruce Coleman Ltd.
105(B) Romi Khosla
106(T) London Daily Mail
106(B) Syndication International Ltd., London
108-9 Gino d'Achille © Aldus Books
110 Royal Geographical Society
111 Popperfoto
112(B) Compix, New York
113(T) Ralph Izzard, The Abominable Snowman Adventure, Hodder & Stoughton Ltd., London
113(CR) Novosti Press Agency
113(B) Chris Bonington/Bruce Coleman Ltd.
114(L) Stamps kindly loaned by Mr. R. A. Topley. Reproduced by permission of the National Postal Museum
114(R) John Francis/Linden Artists © Aldus Books
115(L) John Francis/Linden Artists © Aldus Books after Spectrum
115(R) John Francis/Linden Artists © Aldus Books after Ardea
117 Eastman's Studio
118(T) Compix, New York
118(B) © Aldus Books
120-1 Gino d'Achille © Aldus Books
122, 123(L) John Napier, Bigfoot, © 1972 by John Napier. First published in the U.S.A. by E. P. Dutton & Co., Inc., and reprinted with their permission
123(R) Compix, New York
124 John Napier, Bigfoot, © 1972 by John Napier. First published in the U.S.A. by E. P. Dutton & Co., Inc., and reprinted with their permission
125(R) Compix, New York
126 Courtesy Sabina W. Sanderson and The Society for the Investigation of the Unexplained
127 Raymond Vanker
128-9 Compix, New York
131 Kobal Collection
132 National Portrait Gallery, London
133 Mary Evans Picture Library
134 Kobal Collection
135 Rex Features
136-8 Kobal Collection
139(T) Aldus Archives
139(B) Movie Star News
140-1 National Film Archive
142 Aldus Archives
143 Observer/Transworld